On That Note

SANJAY SUBRAHMANYAN is a singer based in Chennai. A Sangeetha Kalanidhi awardee, his latest album is *Anbenum Peruveli,* which spans genres like blues and rock. This is his first book.

KRUPA GE is a writer based in Chennai. She is the author of a novel, *What We Know About Her* (Context, 2021) and a narrative non-fiction book, *Rivers Remember* (Context, 2019).

SANJAY SUBRAHMANYAN
WITH KRUPA GE

On That Note

Memories of a Life in Music

Published by Westland Non-Fiction, an imprint of Westland Books, a division of Nasadiya Technologies Private Limited, in 2024

No. 269/2B, First Floor, 'Irai Arul', Vimalraj Street, Nethaji Nagar, Alapakkam Main Road, Maduravoyal, Chennai 600095

Westland, the Westland logo, Westland Non-Fiction and the Westland Non-Fiction logo are the trademarks of Nasadiya Technologies Private Limited, or its affiliates.

ISBN: 9789360459673

10 9 8 7 6 5 4 3 2 1

Typeset by Jojy Philip
Printed at [⊠]

Contents

... என்றன்
பாட்டுத் திறத்தாலே – இவ்வையத்தைப்
பாலித்திட வேணும் ...
— சுப்பிரமணிய பாரதி

And with my songs,
Nourish this universe
– Subramania Bharathi

Acknowledgements

The day I was returning from Bangalore with the seed of a book in my mind, I told Aarthi, 'I know who should write this book! It has to be Krupa Ge!' We had read her book *What We Know About Her*, and knew it had all the elements that were so identifiable with my own life in so many ways. Madras, music and the way the world was changing in that landscape. I messaged her on Instagram, and the connect was instantaneous. We did a series of interviews over the next eight to ten months. This was the most exciting part of the book. She came well prepared for every interview. She would read all my blogs and interviews. She had the layout of the book planned perfectly to cover what I wanted to say. She was also persistent where I was reluctant, and drew out the material we needed. I loved the way she eased me into the process of opening up on so many things in my life, including a lot of personal and private reflections on my music and the people around me.

Thanks so so much, Krupa, for being the amazing person that you are!

Thanks to our editor, Ajitha, who has given it this beautiful shape.

Thanks to the publishers for getting me out into the world in this form.

Acknowledgments

CHAPTER 1

The Opening Score

I was on my way back from a concert in Bangalore when my aunt Shobha brought up the idea of a memoir. What would the ten-year-old who wanted to be a cricketer and who devoured Don Bradman's *Farewell to Cricket* think of that, I wondered. Even today the memory feels close—the thrill of finding a dogeared copy of a book written by my idol at the British Council Library where I used to haunt the sports and memoirs section. I could almost picture that Aussie backyard where the Don played cricket using a stump as his makeshift bat. And equally, young Bradman's cricket duels with a curved water tank, which sent the ball bouncing back to him in unpredictable ways. I had long abandoned the bat for a tambura when I read Charlie Chaplin's luminous *My Autobiography* in the 2010s, the other memoir that felt close to the bone. My interest in history and biographies has only grown with the years. So, I told myself I would write one at seventy-five—after all, the comic genius had waited that long to publish his autobiography. Surely I needed at least a few decades more in the arts to be able to talk about my life and work?

Then, a pandemic came; everything changed. Even what I thought of my music. I felt the urge to reflect on my journey, on this metamorphosis, to weigh things up, not just look back at a life lived near the end of it. It felt like an immediate need.

Let me begin with the year 1994. P. Unnikrishnan's gentle voice, singing 'Ennavale' for A.R. Rahman's *Kadhalan* album was everywhere. As word of a singer breaking down barriers between Carnatic music and cinema got around, the questions followed me wherever I went, 'Is it your turn next? Have you received the call yet?' It really was an interesting moment. Here was a traditional Carnatic musician, my contemporary, singing hit playback. There hadn't been any notable crossover between these genres for years. (K.J. Yesudas comes to mind, but then he made the opposite journey. He was a big deal in cinema before he seriously entered the classical stage.)

Through the late 1990s, there were calls aplenty, and I always shied away. From music director Vidyasagar immediately after *Kadhalan*, when I was working as a chartered accountant for Karra & Co., from A.R. Rahman in '98, and later from G.V. Prakash for a song in *Aayirathil Oruvan*. My guru too had been dismissive of the idea then. When Bombay Jayashree and Nithyashree's film songs came out, their popularity soared. Yet, my resolve deepened. I wanted to make it as a pure classical singer.

Ironically, it was receiving the Sangita Kalanidhi—the 'goal', so to speak, as a Carnatic musician—at the relatively young age of forty-seven that made me rethink many deeply held ideas and beliefs. This book is an attempt to explore those early ideas and the rethink. For years, I'd limited myself to Carnatic music, turning down all other opportunities. But I made an about-turn over the past two years. I finally sang my first film song, 'Yedhudhaan Inga Sandhosam', in Sean Roldan's music for the film *Lucky Man* in 2023. I also recorded for Coke Studio Tamil—first, 'Urudhi' in collaboration with Sufi singer Arifullah Shah Rafaee, which was also my first fusion, crossover venture, and later 'Elay Makka' with Andrea Jeremiah, Sathyaprakash, Navz-47 in Girish G.'s music. I have sung an album of Vallalar songs, *Anbenum Peruveli*, featuring genres as varied as blues and rock, and most recently collaborated on a song about Chennai called 'Chennaikaaran' with the inimitable, singer-songwriter Arivu.

On That Note is, in a sense, an attempt at recording this journey as I break genre and change my bio from 'Carnatic musician' to 'singer'. It is, I hope, a reflection on the rationale behind my rethink of a three-decade-long embargo on other musical ventures.

I've drawn a lot of insights over the years from the archiving efforts of others. I obsessively read prefaces to song compilation books, a habit that I can thank the historian V. Sriram for. The preface is where the rich back stories are; how information was gathered, how people met and books were written.

Take, for example, this story I first heard from my guru:

The flautist Thirupampuram Swaminatha Pillai tuned some Muthu Thandavar compositions and presented them to Annamalai University for publication. Around the same time, the teacher-musician Alathur Venkatesa Iyer also set to tune some five songs written by the same sixteenth-century composer in different ragas and presented them to the university. The university set up a committee to deliberate on their publication. Nadaswaram wizard Rajarathnam Pillai and the famous vocalist 'Tiger' Varadachari were in the committee.

Tiger said we'll just publish all the compositions together.

Swaminatha Pillai responded in a huff, 'Either you only publish my thirty-one songs or not at all.'

Annamalai University's 1967 publication of Muthuthandavar's Tamil songs

Rajarathnam Pillai had the last word: 'Swaminatha Pillai's compositions will be published first as they are very good, and the other five songs will be considered for a future publication.'

When I heard this story, I thought maybe this did happen, but who's to know what really transpired? Years went by. I came upon Swaminatha Pillai's book of compositions, and read this very story narrated by the protagonist himself in the preface. Even in the various tellings I had come across, there were some discrepancies in what Rajarathnam Pillai and Tiger actually said, but the larger contours of the story held up.

I mention this to illustrate just how deeply I've been primed to appreciate the printed word. Perhaps this is why, in the early stages of my career, I often engaged with the media. But as years went by, a sense of reluctance crept in. I found myself feeling increasingly uncomfortable during interviews. I got a sense that I was often being probed for controversy rather than for my music. It felt as if a farce was being played out over and over again. So, for instance, I would receive an invitation for an interview ahead of a concert in a city. The questions I was asked would be about the city, my feelings about being there, and so on. There wouldn't be so much as a mention of my concert in the final printed interview. It wasn't so different at home in Chennai either. I would be asked about issues like Chennai's water problems. I was privileged enough to not hold a personal stake in the matter. My building bought water; I was hardly affected by it. How could I say anything meaningful on behalf of those grappling with such a serious issue? The thought that my opinion trivialised the matter upset me. I'd harboured a quiet sense of anger with the press that seemed to not care for Carnatic music anyway. Slowly, over the years, I stopped engaging with the media.

After a decade and a half of silence, I made an exception when I was awarded the Sangita Kalanidhi. Of course, I enjoyed talking to the handful of writers who took the trouble to listen to my music, but I couldn't shake off the feeling that the media was static.

This was why, during the pandemic, I finally decided to breathe music into my YouTube channel. I had spent the first six months of 2020 believing that stage performances would make a quick comeback. Even as digital concerts became the norm, I felt that my identity was intrinsically linked to live performances. So I refused to sing for an online audience. My wife Aarthi, who has been video recording all of my concerts since 2012, gently nudged me towards an alternative. She suggested we upload one recording from our video archives online every day; thanks to her efforts, 150 of my concert songs are out there on YouTube now.

Months went by in 2020 with no change. Not even in my wildest dreams did I imagine a 'virtual music season' would come to pass in my lifetime. But after nearly a year of COVID-19, December presented a new normal, and I played along. Month-long classical recitals and lec-dems that sprawled across the city's cultural spaces, that was the music season I grew up with. It had suddenly shrunk into an online affair. By then, the high of performing for a live audience had been replaced by a solitary ritual—singing kutcheris to myself at home. Motivation was hard to muster, but I persisted, gritting my teeth. There was always the hope that things might improve swiftly, and one had to be ready. So, I kept practising.

In an interview to Larry King, pop singer Celine Dion once described her routine with a voice coach as 'really boring ... very boring' even as she demonstrated her warm-up in earnest. A seasoned stock trader will confirm that 60 per cent of the time the market moves in a predictable range, 'the usual boring stuff'. The most successful fast bowlers invest more time on their dreary drills every day than they do actually bowling those dazzling outswingers. It's the same with Carnatic music. When someone asks me 'How do you practise? It must be great to listen to you at home?', my answer is, 'Sorry, but it's just boring stuff'. Listening to phrases and songs repeatedly can get extremely tedious. Aarthi still has nightmares about the third swaram of a particular varnam I found tough to crack nearly twenty-five years ago. On tours, I have seen this happen with violinist Varadarajan and mridangist Venkatesh. Varadu would repeat some difficult phrases one hundred times, even as Venkatesh persisted with 'tha ka tharikita thaka' on his thighs over and over again, while we were on the way to the concert. This is why we all practise as if we're quarantining; to spare each other the burdens of our 'boring stuff'.

From March to mid-November in 2020, my routine was just this boring stuff. And yet, it was meaningful for I finally found time to dig into more compositions, set songs to tune and even introspect on the form and content of my music. The transition to virtual concerts finally brought some changes to my routine. That year's 'season' featured pre-recorded kutcheris which were streamed on different dates. We made our way through it, our fingers crossed in the hope of returning to performance sooner than later.

In the meantime, as the pandemic raged on, I sought connection through that digital void with audiences, reaching out over Facebook, the pages of my blog, Instagram and Twitter. I was actually an early social media user. I'd been on it from when Facebook and Twitter were used for quaint things like exchanging information about each other (and not for trolling or baiting!).

Then the 2021 music season came, and with it empty auditoriums. This silence finally prompted another decision—digital concerts with my own banner, Sanjay Sabha Live. I was happy to be finally singing. We recorded one virtual concert each month for my YouTube channel. The challenge of doing things in a new way was exciting. Even an ordinarily straightforward event like the soundcheck now looked different. Earlier, I would sing for about fifteen minutes while experienced technicians got it all done.

I would use this time for additional warm-up, singing a few lines of sangathi, and to acquaint myself with the ambience. Archaic equipment or subpar acoustics did come in the way of this quick setting-up, and some human factors contributed to delays as well, but then I couldn't really complain as I too have caused delays.

Filming virtual concerts, on the other hand, was truly complex. Besides sound, we also grappled with issues of lighting and camera angles. New venues meant new challenges, demanding adaptability. We needed to stay patient, given the stress of the pandemic weighing on everyone's shoulders. The accompanists and I powered through those months, performing virtually even when live concerts slowly resumed by the end of 2021, even as 2022 brought more uncertainties, with the number of cases surging and waning.

It is difficult to put into words the feeling of euphoria one experienced when a concert was fixed in the COVID years, and the crash that came when one heard that it had been postponed, or worse, cancelled.

I had been a performing artist for most of my life, and all my personal musical ups and downs came from the live concert experience. When I had no choice, I finally began to enjoy the digital space. Bhargavii Mani, the orchestrator of my new virtual stage, suggested we expand beyond performance. And that is really the origin story of 'On That Note', which began as a segment on my YouTube channel where I shared stories of my encounters with ragas and musicians over two seasons. I approached Bhargavii during the later stages of the pandemic to help fix my online presence. She was instrumental in giving my digital space the look and feel it has today. Over the last three years, she produced all the episodes of 'On That Note', 'Short Notes' and 'Sanjay Sabha' on YouTube. Initially, I was very diffident in front of the camera, but she encouraged me, and through repeated iterations, she trained me to feel more comfortable and be myself on screen. This work also made later ventures, like Coke Studio, much easier for me.

Another big influence on my life and music trajectory was Thyagu thaatha, my maternal grandfather; his storytelling style shaped mine too. I remember lunch hour being a riot, when he treated my brother Shyam, cousin Boo and me to epics with his own twist. One story, vivid even now, unfolded like a web series, featuring Duryodhana's hunt for the Pandavas in exile, Shakuni's sinister plots to aid him and Krishna's divine interventions. Mottayan, a fictional eagle created by my thaatha, and his feathered friends added layers to this story. My amma had inherited his flair; her tales too drew an audience of wide-eyed children at lunch hour. When my turn came, my daughter Shreyasi became the enchanted listener to stories starring CID Ramki and his trusty assistant Sivaramakrishnan—my homage to Sherlock and Watson. Familiar faces from our lives played starring roles in these stories; Varadarajan and Venkatesh were recurring characters.

At home and with the world at large, I have enjoyed sharing my stories. While my blog, Instagram, YouTube, Twitter and Facebook offer glimpses, I've felt that I'm both sharing and scattering my thoughts. The social media landscape lacks the cohesion of a book. So here I am, on that note, telling you, my reader, the whole story, from the beginning, as I continue in my grandfather's and mother's footsteps, narrating the story of my life thus far.

CHAPTER 2

It Takes a Village to Raise a Musician

I was born on 21 January 1968. Amma apparently attended every concert at the Music Academy—Carnatic music's unofficial headquarters—the month before. Everyone at home joked that she was going to have me in the lobby of the Academy.

My early years, though, were spent in Calcutta, where Appa's job as a service engineer for Philips took our family. My paternal grandparents, Subrahmanyan and Bhagyam, lived in Calcutta as well in those days. My grandmother, a veena player, had a great influence on my childhood. Besides card games and chess, she also taught me the art of identifying ragas by comparing them to songs I knew.

We rebounded to Madras when I was in class two, in December 1974, and my first real encounter with music would come as soon as 1975. Our music-loving family was thrilled to move back home, that too to the Royapettah area, just one street away from classical music royalty, Semmangudi Srinivasa Iyer.

My maternal grandparents, Thyagu and Lakshmi, spent a lot of time with us. My paatti had learnt to play the violin from a grandson of Thirukodikaval Krishna Iyer and hailed from the same village. She loved the music of M.D. Ramanathan, but her heart belonged to M.S. Subbulakshmi. Whenever she heard a song, she needed to know what raga it was, what its parent raga was—essentially, what its origins were. She was always looking for musical knowledge. This would manifest in her later years, as her memory began to wane, in amusing ways. She would insist that whatever raga I was speaking to her about was originally called something else. I never could figure out then if she was recalling some academic debates or if she was confused. She would sometimes forget even my mother, but she never forgot me. And if she saw me, she had to talk about music.

When I was just two, Amma took me to a Lalgudi Jayaraman concert, where apparently, I announced, 'I'll play the violin like him one day.' She never forgot, and brought it up when we moved back home. Amma asked me in all earnestness, 'Would you like to learn to play the violin, da?', and was met with emphatic agreement. Her inquiries led Amma to V. Lakshminarayana Iyer, who was renowned for teaching children. Amma didn't wait for the Vijayadashami date, as was custom, to initiate me into the arts. To my teacher's credit, nor did he. And so my first formal music class was in the spring of 1975. I can't quite remember the exact date, though I still have the book with my very first lesson, sarali varisai, in my teacher's writing. He believed that one must know to sing what one plays—be it sarali varisai, janta varisai or keerthanams—and so had me bowing strings and singing along.

My mother, who had learnt under Flute Rajarama Iyer in Mayavaram and later from Mayavaram Saraswathy, would sing every day at home. Not formally with a sruti box, but while cooking and doing other housework. By the time I started learning music at the age of seven, I could sing most of those songs by heart. She conducted Chinmaya Mission's Bala Vihar classes at home, immersing me in bhajans, slokas and stories from an early age. When I was in the fifth grade, I narrated the entire Ramayana and Mahabharatha to my Moral Science class, filling the last ten minutes of the period over several days, thanks to her.

All of Amma's siblings learnt music from Saraswathy too. My uncle played the flute and all my aunts sang. I naturally joined them (and my thaatha who too could sing) soon. For seven years, I learnt to sing as well as play the violin, twice a week, and that remained my main connection to the world of classical music.

But I wanted to listen to music at all times of the day. Growing up, if I could get my hands on it, I heard it ... records, LPs, my father's spool tapes. I spent summers in Calcutta through the late seventies listening to every gramophone record in my paternal grandparents' vast, terrific collection when I went to visit them. I still remember this one Natabhairavi Ragam Tanam Pallavi (RTP) of Balamuralikrishna's that I heard several times on those hot afternoons. It was the only thing I could do to pass time then. There was no one around but my grandparents; the kids next door would have gone to school. To begin with, I was preoccupied with figuring out how to operate the record player, and my grandparents didn't mind. My interest in music followed naturally.

Our house was just a few streets away from the Academy. In the mid-seventies, after finishing a game of street cricket, my friends would ask if I wanted to go to a kutcheri. Back then, I knew almost no musicians, but they did. They took me to hear T.R. Subramaniam. They even hyped up TRS to me to make me go. 'It will be really entertaining,' they promised. He had a very engaging way of singing swarams. And so I started tagging along with them. By the late seventies and eighties, I eagerly awaited 1 December, when all the sabhas in the city would publish their concert lists for the music season. My father would type out the season's concert details, cyclostyle them and distribute copies to his friends for free.

The big conversations at home were always about who had been promoted to the afternoon or evening slots that year and which big accompanists were playing—with names like Mani Iyer and Trichy Sankaran being mentioned often.

My main curiosity in those years was about who my guru's sons were accompanying at the Academy. Back then, his elder son, L. Subramaniam, the classical musician and composer, played violin for vocalist K.V. Narayanaswamy, and his other son, L. Shankar, a.k.a Shenkar, who was also in the fusion band Shakti with John Mclaughlin, played for senior musician Madurai Somu. I even attended a concert in 1979 at the Academy where Shenkar was accompanying Somu; C.S. Murugabhoopathy was on the mridangam. During an RTP in the raga Swarnangi, as Shenkar began his turn of the alapana and moved on to the upper shadja, Somu stopped and asked him to play a bit more in the panchamam range. I had never heard a main artist, a singer, tell the violin accompanist 'play for some more time, it's very nice' on stage. I still haven't. But hearing Somu say this to Shenkar, *my* guru's son, was a thrill for my young self.

Until 1982, my focus had remained the violin. That year, my guru emigrated to America to join Subramaniam. Before leaving, he'd suggested I continue learning the violin from Thiruparkadal Veeraraghavan, whose father and he had learnt music together. But my maternal grandaunt, Rukmini Rajagopalan, who was a singer, was not very keen on this course of action. Family discussions about potential gurus for me constantly met with vetoes. Meanwhile, we moved homes. And so, for about half a year in 1982, my music and I were in limbo.

It was Amma once again who initiated my journey back to the violin. She adored M.L. Vasanthakumari's music, and so, on a whim one morning she took me straight to the home of MLV's long-time accompanist, the accomplished Kanyakumari. (As an aside, we love addressing musicians by their initials and making acronyms of names here in the Carnatic world. So Vasanthakumari is MLV, Subbulakshmi is MS, Balasubramaniam is GNB. It's a quirk even filmmaker Balachander couldn't resist. In his 1975 film *Apoorva Ragangal,* his Carnatic music singing protagonist (played by MLV's daughter Srividya) is 'MRB'.)

That day, during my visit to Kanyakumari's house, she asked me, 'Why don't you play what you know and show?' I did. Feedback came swiftly—'Why are you not playing the gamakas well? I will teach you; practice at home.'

This is how I came to learn music from the veteran for two sessions. Her fee though, Rs 75 for eight classes, which was a considerable sum for our family in 1982, prompted Amma to have a frank conversation with me. I was fourteen then, and she could tell me about her constraints.

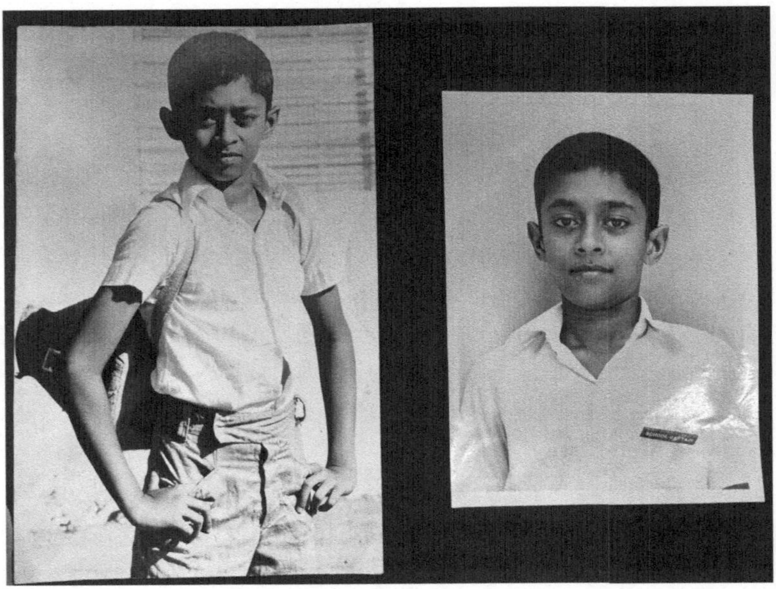

Those cricket-crazy school days

'Promise you'll practise for two hours every day, I'll find a way to send you to Kanyakumari.'

I was frank as well. 'No way. I have to play cricket; I have other interests. I won't do it.'

That was that.

Meanwhile, Rukmini paati encouraged me to sing, so I began learning from her daughter, my aunt Sukanya Swaminathan, twice or thrice a week. This is around when my voice broke. I'd been singing at five (G) kattai, and suddenly I was at one and a half (C Sharp) kattai.

In those years, ghatam player Umalayapuram Narayanaswamy lived in the house above ours. One day, when his friend, the violinist M.S. Anantharaman, visited, their conversation somehow turned to the young boy downstairs who sang and played the violin. I was called upstairs for a quick showcase.

'You are playing well enough, why did you let the violin go?'

When he heard about my predicament, Anantharaman offered, 'I will send a boy to teach you.' He kept his word and dispatched T.S. Seshadri, his student from the music college, who is now at Rishi Valley, to my house. He taught me for six months, but my practice routine remained very inconsistent. And then, in an accident at school during a high jump, I ended up with a fracture in my arm, which made even holding the violin painful. That put paid to my playing.

My singing class with Sukanya athai was the only constant through it all. This was the mid-eighties, when Amma also took me to several music competitions.

In 1984, to my own surprise, I received the consolation prize at a Music Academy contest. At this point, Rukmini paati stepped in and offered to personally train me for contests. I started going to her more regularly.

Rukmini paati belonged to a time when cricket still distinguished between Gentlemen and Players. And she identified as an amateur—a Gentlewoman, not a Player. She spoke of several people like her in the musical community. These amateurs were either family women, most of whom sang only on the radio, or corporate executives who also performed regularly on the radio. As far as performing skills were concerned, there was not much of a difference between these amateurs and successful professional concert artists. The main difference was that the amateurs were perfectly happy being just that, singing their radio concert once every two months. They never aspired to sing at major sabhas or music festivals. The amateurs would probably sing at the odd family wedding, maybe after the muhurtham—the wedding ceremony—before lunch was served, or during or after the nalangu (post-wedding) rituals and maybe after the nischayatharthham, the formal engagement. They'd leave the main reception concert to those pros.

I liked singing, I always have. But I never thought back then, even when I was learning from my athai, that I would sing a kutcheri in the near future. That I would become a Player.

After my tenth standard at St Bede's, I transferred to Vidya Mandir. I was in a completely different cultural milieu all of a sudden, even though both schools were in the Mylapore area. St Bedes was a convent, Vidya Mandir was predominantly brahmin. St Bedes was (and continues to be) famous for cricket. My Anglo-Indian classmates who made up the light music troupe there were very sceptical of my ability to hold a tune. I still remember a senior from St Bedes named Bharani, who would win every singing competition. His voice hadn't broken and was very melodious. At a school reunion recently, many of us reminisced about his stunning performance of 'Oru Iniya Manadhu' from the Rajinikanth-Sridevi hit movie *Johnny*. All my friends ragged me about losing to him in contests, as they always have. I reminded them that I finally beat him one year with the retro Chandrababu song, 'Kalyanam ha ha ha kalyanam'. Until I was in the eleventh standard, I harboured this desire to sing in films. I even wanted to join light-music troupes.

At Vidya Mandir, though, there seemed to be a dearth of singers, and I found myself participating in school-level cultural competitions with my new friends, the Sriram duo—Sriram Krishnan, violin maestro T.N. Krishnan's son, and Sriram Gangadharan, a flautist, one year junior to me. We became a team because the senior boys in the twelfth standard saw an opportunity to boost the school's standing in culturals when they figured out that all three of us were learning music.

'If you go, we could even lay our hands on the championship because we get points only for dumb charades and quiz now,' they said. But to proceed, we needed the principal's permission, because in those days Vidya Mandir had prohibited light-music troupes! When the principal found out we were Carnatic musicians forming a classical music group, and was assured that there was not even a guitar involved, she gave us the green light.

There was still a problem. I did not know how to sing kalpana swaram back then, and both Srirams were good enough to play concerts. Percussion was by a guy called N.V. Shankar, who played the tabla. He had a good instinct for rhythm and could follow anything that we played. We were hardly sixteen at the time, but one of us was T.N. Krishnan's son after all, and the other had had his flute arangetram at eight in Delhi. The boys volunteered to coach me in singing improvisations. We figured no one would sing kalpana swaram at an eleventh-standard music competition and practised hard, with korappu volleys to boot, for three months. Then we started winning. Our repertoire was just three songs: 'Nera Nammithi', the ata tala varnam, the famous 'Vatapi Ganapatim' and the English Note 'Ga Ma Ga Ri Ga Pa'. Whether the competition spanned five minutes with just Vatapi, three minutes featuring only the Note, a more elaborate twelve-minute rendition incorporating all three, or twenty minutes, where we performed the varnam in three speeds, we always won. Winning these school-level contests gave me my first taste of that musical high I would spend my life chasing.

I did have some stage fright as a child, but it seemed to fade away quickly. I was in class six when I got on stage for the first time for an elocution competition. Appa had taught me the

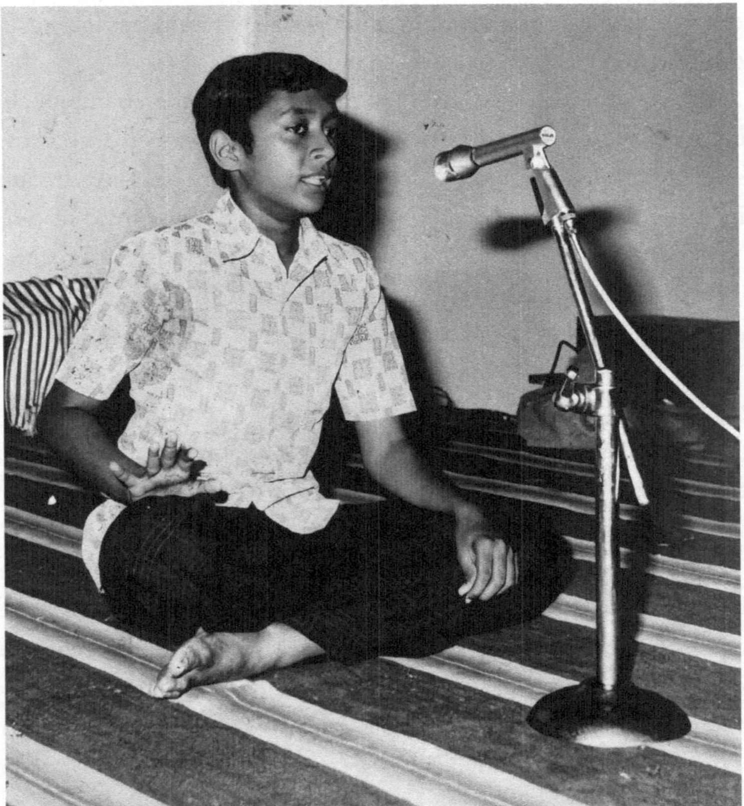

Early concert look

'Friends, Romans, countrymen' speech; I was Marc Antony. I still remember my legs quaking, going thud-thud on stage. But then I ended up winning that contest, and by the next year I was ready for the stage.

That was also the year audio cassettes from TDK came out in a big way. Spool tapes were on their way out. Appa suggested I convert his tape collection into cassettes when I was free, but his tape recorder wasn't working. We were living in the Abhiramapuram neighbourhood, and coincidentally, the house behind ours belonged to my future wife Aarthi's family. Her father, Srinivasan, and my Appa had been colleagues at Philips. She also happened to be my brother's classmate. I walked into their house unannounced to borrow my father's friend Srinivasan's tape recorder. It's almost unthinkable today, visiting someone's home without at least a phone call to warn them. But that was a different time, I guess. My future father-in-law handed his precious Grundig tape recorder over when he learnt I was Sankaran's son.

Appa and I set up the equipment. And my project began in earnest. The first tape I converted was a recording of G.N. Balasubramaniam's concert for Perambur Sangeetha Sabha. He sang an ethereal 'Maragadavallim', set in Kambhoji raga. *That* was the transformative moment; something clicked inside of me when I heard that GNB recording, and then I knew I had to sing. I had just learnt that very Dikshitar composition from Rukmini paati. I immersed myself in that Kambhoji, listening to it repeatedly, practising the sangathis and swaras.

That year, during this spool tape–conversion project, I listened to a great deal of music. My days, in fact, were all about music. At home I was doing this, and at school I was practising with the troupe. We were soon able to expand our repertoire, and the boys would demand, 'Dei sing this raga, da!' I would sing the raga, Sriram would sing swaras that I couldn't, I would practice. This is

AIR music competition prize winners

NEW DELHI, Oct. 10.

Miss Sangrami Chatterjee of Calcutta and Miss Kalyani Panchapakesan of Madras have won the first prizes among girls in the All India Radio music competition, 1986, in the Hindustani and Carnatic categories, respectively.

A total of 23 boys and girls have been awarded prizes in the competition, the results of which were announced here on Friday.

Thirteen of them have won prizes for Hindustani music and 10 for Carnatic music. There are some categories wherein no awards have been given, an official press release stated.

Hindustani music: Girls: Vocal: Classical (khayal)—Miss Sangrami Chatterjee (first), Miss Rini Choudhury of Calcutta (second). In the boys section no award was given.

Vocal: Light classical—No first prize, Miss Sangeeta Adhikary of Calcutta (second). No award for boys.

Vocal: Light—Boys: Dinesh Kumar Kantha of Simla in ghazal (first), Kaushik Kumar Srimal of Ahmedabad in bhajans and geets (second). Girls: Miss Swagataluxmi Dasgupta of Calcutta (first), Miss Manasi Mukherjee of Calcutta (second). Miss Dasgupta also won the first prize in vocal Rabindra Sangeet.

Plucked instruments (except veena): Debashish Bhattacharya of Calcutta (sarod) (first), Madan Oak of Pune (santoor) (second).

Percussion instruments (except pakhwaj): Kubernath Mishra of Varanasi (tabla) (first), Debasish Roy of Calcutta (tabla) (second).

Vocal: Classical—Boys: S. Subrahmanyan of Madras (first). Girls: Miss Kalyani Panchapakesan of Madras (first), Miss S. Visalakshi of Madras (second).

Vocal: Light classical—Boys: No first prize, K. Muralidharan Unni of Trichur (second). Girls: Miss P. E. Geetha of Bombay (first), Miss V. Kalavathi of Bangalore (second).

Vocal: Light—Boys: P. S. Anil Kumar of Trichur (first). Among girls Miss Lalithakshari of Madras (first) and Miss N. C. Suvarana of Bangalore (second).

String instruments (bowed): Miss Kalyani Panchapakesan of Madras (violin) (first).

String instruments (plucked): Miss Jayasree Ravindran of Bombay (veena) (first).

Percussion instruments: C. N. Balaji of Bombay (mridangam) and V. V. Vaidyanathan of Trichur (second).

Wind instruments: V. Magaraj of Hyderabad (first). Nadaswaram (special prize): G. Kothandaraman of Madras.—PTI

THE HINDU — 11—10—1986

That all-important AIR winner announcement

how, with a little help from my friends, I learnt the intricacies of kalpana swaram and manodharma singing. While my grandaunt was great at teaching keerthanams and ragas, she hadn't been able to teach me swaras. It was these boys who also introduced me to concepts like kanakku and tisram. I began to look forward to my Sundays with them.

In 1986, I won an All India Radio competition and was conferred a B grade; that was the first prize. It meant I had to perform. Until then, I hadn't sung a concert, hadn't got on a stage with accompanists. All I had under my belt were these competitions. Then, Carnatic singer Vijay Siva reached out to me, insisting I perform a kutcheri for the Youth Association for Classical Music (YACM). I told him I was just eighteen, a stage novice.

He said, 'Nothing doing. You've been awarded a B grade, you have to sing a half-hour concert for the radio anyway; this is just another hour and a half. Practise and you'll be able to do it.'

When my grandaunt found out, she said it was a mistake too. 'What's the hurry? There's so much more for him to learn,' she warned.

Eventually, Vijay Siva prevailed. He arranged for my very first concert at a Pillayar temple. Following four months of rigorous practice, I sang my first kutcheri. The song list featured ragas Bhairavi and Mohanam, Rukmini paati's favourites. The concert was well received, and I was even reviewed in the Tamil daily *Dinamani*. Two more concert invites followed swiftly. That December was my third concert, though not as part of the season. By nineteen, I was singing concerts regularly. I'd arrived at that moment where I could say, *oh, maybe I do have a chance at this, at becoming a vidwan*.

I finished school in 1986. I had long decided that science wasn't for me, it was going to be commerce as I wanted to do chartered accountancy. A day college seat was very competitive, but I secured the Vivekananda College evening B.Com. slot quite easily. I remember being overjoyed at this. All my mornings would now be for music. I would go to Sriram's house, and we'd practise, or he would come to mine. (Sriram Krishnan had left for Delhi by then; Sriram Gangadharan and I met on weekdays and Sundays too.) I had also made other musician friends, who played the mridangam and violin, and they would show up, and we would all play together. Finally, it dawned on me that it was just a matter of time, that music and singing were going to be my career.

The Tamil Nadu Eyal Isai Nataka Manram (EINM) had a great scheme for promoting musical and dancing talents in those days. One applied for the fellowship as an individual, and the Manram would put together a team of three to four applicant artists who had also qualified. They would all get a chance to perform at four different venues in Tamil Nadu, one of which was always Chennai. Sabhas from all over the state would register with the EINM, and they were allotted artists to perform. In 1987-88, I was selected. The acceptance letter I wrote to the organisers was perhaps the first official letter I'd written in Tamil (unless you count the letter-writing question that I attempted in my tenth-standard public exam).

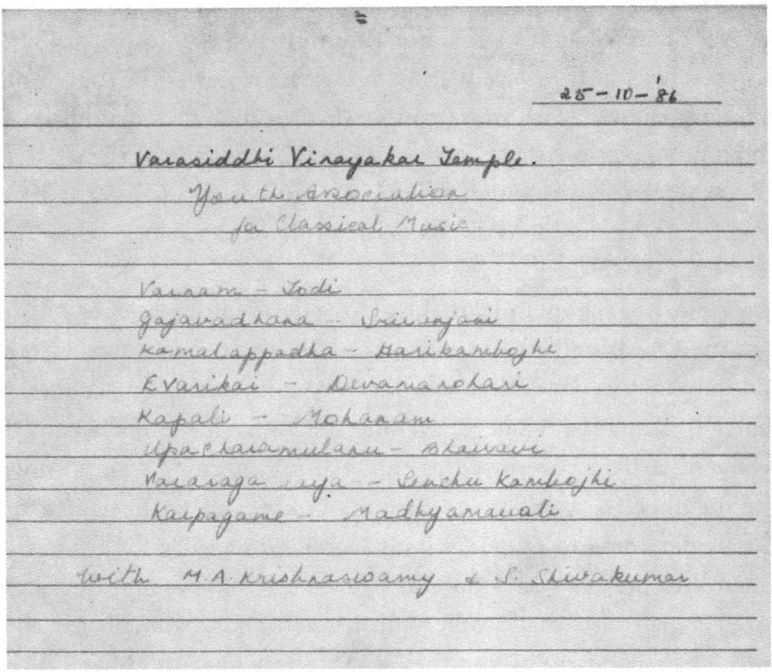

25-10-'86

Varasiddhi Vinayakar Temple.
Youth Association
for Classical Music.

Varnam - Todi
Gajavadhana - Sriranjani
Kamalappadha - Harikambojhi
Evarikai - Devamanohari
Kapali - Mohanam
Upacharamulanu - Bhairavi
Nararaga riya - Sencha Kambojhi
Karpagame - Madhyamavati

with M.A. Krishnaswamy & S. Shivakumar

My very first concert's song list

When my letter arrived, I found out that my former violin teacher T.S. Seshadri, along with Kovai G. Prakash on mridangam, would be my accompanists. Seshadri had just finished studying at the Madras Music College, and was playing concerts and freelancing as a teacher then. I was thrilled to reconnect with him, this time as the main artist, with my former teacher, who was more like a senior friend, playing with me.

The first concert was at Gobichettipalayam. Seshadri and I reached Erode and took a bus to the venue. We had to stay in the groom's room of a wedding hall where the concert was to be held—the title 'Mappillai' in Tamil was inscribed outside our room. Seshadri had warned me that any number above ten in the audience would be a new record for the sabha. We had a whole day to kill and went to see a film, *Michael Raj*, starring Raghuvaran and Madhuri. Later in the afternoon, Prakash joined us from Coimbatore and we had ourselves a great time discussing GNB. Prakash was also very good at mimicking the top mridangists of the day. As expected, the audience was nine in number, but I managed to sing a two-hour concert and made my way back home with Rs 225.

The next concert was in Sastry Hall, Chennai, for the Saraswati Vaggeyakara Trust. As I began my todi alapana, in walked flute maestro Hariprasad Chaurasia and the tabla player Anindo Chatterjee. My cousin, who was organising Hariji's concert for Spic Macay had brought them there. Chaurasia graciously stayed until the end and even offered his blessings.

Seshadri, Prakash and I then travelled to Thiruvaiyaru to perform at the Tamil Isai Sangam, and then to RR Sabha in Trichy. The Sangam had insisted I sing only Tamil songs, I remember. At the venue, I met nadaswaram artist Vyasarpadi Kothandaraman who had also won the AIR competition in 1986. He was there with his elder brother E. Uthirakumar, who played with another brother E. Haridas. Their stage name was 'Thiruppulivanam brothers'. Uthirakumar gave me a quiet but brilliant lesson that day as we all sat together. He'd asked me to sing raga Huseni and I said to him that I couldn't, that it was hard. 'Ada, summa sa pa sa vecchu paadunga!' Just keep singing the notes sa pa sa, Huseni, will come

Phone : 451669

SARASWATHI

57, ROSTREVOR,

MADRAS-600 018.

9-2-88 (Tuesday)

&

10-2-88 (Wednesday)

Lecture Demonstration on

"Carnatic Music Prior to Trinity"

by

Sri S. R. Janakiraman

accompanied by

Sri C. Lakshminarayanan	— Violin
Sri T. K. Ramakrishnan	— Mridangam

11-2-88 (Thursday)

Sponsored by

Tamil Nadu Eyal Isai Nataka Manram

Sri S. Subramanian	— Vocal
Sri T. S. Seshadri	— Violin
Kovai Sri G. Prakash	— Mridangam

27-2-88 (Saturday)

Selvi Lathangi Ramanathan	— Vocal
Selvi M. K. Padmini	— Violin
Sri N. Mohan	— Mridangam

Venue : SRINIVASA SASTRI HALL, LUZ.

Time : 6-45 p. m.

Concert announcement from my first tour

through. That was a eureka moment—nobody had explained that raga like this to me until then. He even sang for us using the three notes for five minutes that day. I remember being blown away by how he'd explained this and the way the raga came together then. Even now, every time I sing Huseni, I remember his lesson.

The next day we performed in Trichy's RR sabha to a decent crowd. As I was singing the main item, Unnikrishnan entered the hall. He had finished performing in Karur and was spending the day in Trichy. I cancelled my return ticket, hung out with Unni and we returned by bus the next day.

It was my first time seeing Tamil Nadu beyond Madras. Buying the ticket, getting the concession forms filled out, travelling to smaller towns, walking around and soaking in the sights and landscape, I loved every bit of it. Even though the crowds at these concerts were often disappointing, performing at each venue was still an important experience in that early stage in my career. Singing, experimenting on stage, working with accompanists—I enjoyed all of it. Meeting musical friends, discussing ragas, jamming, learning, asking them what they'd recently learnt, discussing kanakku and listening to tapes, this was the world I was part of.

That first tour seemed to have set something in motion. It was the perfect lead-in to 1988—a year that was all kinds of significant. It was the year I performed for the first time at Ragapriya, one of the most interesting sabhas in Madurai. The concert was held in the ballroom of the Pandyan Hotel. The audience was incredibly appreciative, but they also had some fascinating customs. For starters, concerts had to be at least three hours long. Most of the audience sat on the floor, with just a few chairs tucked away at the back. There were no microphones; these were true chamber concerts, and the crowd took pride in that. Perhaps the most striking tradition was that they didn't clap after individual songs. Instead, at the very end of the concert they would give the performers a single ovation, something I found very charming. It was also in 1988 that the Music Academy started the first Spirit of Youth concerts in memory of composer Ambujam Krishnaa. There was already a buzz around the YACM, and Vijay Siva, who was its president, was singing to a full house in the 12 p.m. slot by then. Thanks to the YACM, I was finally initiated to the Music Academy stage, where I sang for an hour, alongside singers Nithyashree and Balaji Shankar. That year, I recall, the festival also hosted one-and-a-half-hour-long concert sessions with artists a little senior to me, like Unnikrishnan and Anuradha Sriram.

It was also the year my name became Sanjay Subrahmanyan.

Most people spell 'Sanjay' the right way, though there was the odd 'Sanjai' printed in some concert invites. But the 'Subrahmanyan' has been spelt as Subrahmanyam, Subrahmaniyam, Subrahmaniam, Subhramaniam, Subramaniam, Subramanian, Subramoneyam, Subramoniam, and I could go on and on and on. People ask me all the time why I spell it this way. Is it numerology? No. It was the way my paternal grandfather spelt his name. And he just passed it on to me. He was a music enthusiast only through his association with my grandmother's family but had his own distinct tastes. He adored M.D. Ramanathan and the Sama raga. And apparently, if his name were to be correctly transliterated from its Sanskrit original, then this would be it. My grandfather was quite insistent that his name be spelt exactly, and famously returned letters that misspelt it. He even wrote a letter to my second-standard class teacher asking her to change the spelling of my name in the report card she had prepared. Though I spell my name the same as my grandfather, I really cannot insist on it the way he did. Imagine if I rejected concert invitations that came my way because my name was misspelt? I'd be better off in another profession. I'm just grateful for all the people that do try and retain my original spelling.

In truth, my given name was 'Subrahmanyan', and all my academic life I was known as S. Subrahmanyan, with the initial standing for 'Sankaran', my father's name. 'Sanjay' was just what I was called at home. My school and college friends still call me 'Subra'. My first concert in 1986 too was advertised as 'S. Subrahmanyan – Vocal'. In 1988, the late S.V. Krishnan of the famous Raga Sudha Hall invited me to Coimbatore for a concert. He was in the process of shifting to Chennai but still ran his Raga Sudha Sabha in Coimbatore. I don't know who told him what, but the invitation to my concert came with the name 'Sanjay Subrahmanyan – Vocal'. That name just stuck. (And now, whenever people come up to me and ask me if my father is Mr Subrahmanyan, I have to tell them this whole story.)

The following year, 1989, brought me my first December music season kutcheri at the revered Academy.

Thus far, my gurus had all taught me in their own ways. My violin teacher had prepared me to play for concerts, so I could immediately graduate when I started singing. I learnt from Sukanya athai for about two years. She helped me prepare for contests, taught me Swati Thirunal songs and trained me in raga alapanas. Then I moved to learning from her mother, my grandaunt. Between 1984 and '89, she focused on deepening my understanding of ragas and keerthanams.

Then I met KSK (K.S. Krishnamurthy) maama. His son K.K. Ravi, who passed away in 1991 in an accident, was one of my closest friends. I had met Ravi through YACM. He was a brilliant violinist, Lalgudi's student, and had accompanied me in many concerts. He introduced me to his father. My grandmother Bhagyam knew KSK maama from her time in Calcutta, and my

DHINAMANI — 11-11-1986

கலை அரங்கம்

★ ★ ★

"சாஸ்திரீய சங்கீதத்திற்கான இளைஞர் சங்கத்தின் ஆதரவில் அண்மையில் பெசண்ட்நகர் விநாயகர் ஆலய மண்டபத்தில் இளைஞர் எஸ்.பாலசுப்பிரமணியத்தின் இன்னிசை நடைபெற்றது. இந் நிகழ்ச்சியில் எம்.ஏ.கிருஷ்ணசுவாமி வயலினும், எஸ்.சிவகுமார் மிருதங்கமும் வாசித்தனர்.

ருக்மிணி ராஜகோபாலனிடம் இசை பயின்றிருக்கும் சுப்பிரமண்யத்திற்கு ரஞ்சகமான சாரீரம். சாரீரத்தில் நல்ல உதவுப்படியும், அழுத்தமும், கமகமும் காணப்படுகின்றன. வல்லினம், மெல்லினம் கொடுத்து அழகாகப் பாடுகிறார்.

நிகழ்ச்சியை 'தோடி' ராக (எராநாபை) வர்ணத்துடன் சுப்பிரமண்யம் தொடங்கினார். பாபநாசம் சிவனின் "கஜவதன" (ஸ்ரீரஞ்சனி) "கமலபத மலரினை" (ஹரி காம்போதி) இவ்விரு கிருதிகளையும் அடுத்தடுத்து வழங்கிவிட்டு அன்றைய முதல் ராகமான "தேவமனோஹரியை" (எவரிகை) சுருக்கமாக ஆலாபனை செய்த போதிலும், ராக ஆலாபனை முதல் தரமாகவே இருந்தது. அடுத்து மோகன ராகத்தை சிறப்பாக ஆலாபனை செய்ததுடன் பாபநாசம் சிவனின் 'காபாலி' கிருதியின் பல்லவியில் கச்சிதமாக ஸ்வரப்ரஸ்தாரமும் செய்தார். அன்றைய பிரதான ராகமான 'பைரவி'யை (உபசாரமு) மூன்று ஸ்தாயிகளிலும் படிப்படியாக விரிவுபடுத்தி பாவப் பெருக்குடன் ஆலாபனை செய்தது விதரணையுடன் விளங்கியது. 'உபசாரமு' கிருதியில் "கபட நாடக சூத்ர தாரிவை" என்ற இடத்தில் செய்த நிரவலும் ஸ்வரப்பிரஸ்தாரமும் நிறைவுடன் காணப்பட்டன.

பக்க வாத்யம் வாசித்த கிருஷ்ணசுவாமியும், சிவகுமாரும் அனுசரணையாக வாசித்து சிறப்பித்தனர். மிருதங்கம் வாசித்த இளைஞர் சிவகுமார் நமது கவனத்தை வெகுவாக கவர்ந்தார். வைதீச்வரன் கோவில் வைத்யநாதனின் சீடரான (இடது கை வாகு கொண்ட) இவரது கையில் அழுத்தம், காலப்பிரமாண சுத்தம் இவை நன்கு அமையப் பெற்றிருக்கின்றன. திடமான தன்னம்பிக்கையுடன் சுகமாக வாசிக்கிறார். அவரது அன்றைய ஆதி தாளம் இரண்டு களை முக்கால் இடத்திற்கான தனியும் அப்போது கையாண்ட திச்ர அமைப்புகளும் சுவையுடன் காணப்பட்டன.

When a review mistakenly referred to me as Balasubramaniam uncle, Suresh, had learnt music from him in Calcutta. Suresh chittappa was so good that everyone in my family felt he should have performed as a professional. But he shied away from the Chennai scene as he lived in Calcutta, and chose to work in the branding and advertising industry. When I started going to KSK maama, it was if the baton had been passed, and when I started singing, Suresh chittappa also began coming down for the music season more regularly to listen.

I was in my early twenties at this point, and there were some challenges to learning from a family elder, some moments of friction. Understandably, I didn't find everything my grandaunt said agreeable, and sometimes I'd get angry and leave in a huff. When I said I wanted to learn a song in Kedaragowla raga once, she said she didn't know any. When I suggested KSK maama's name, she agreed immediately, 'Go and learn from him.' But when I sang something else I'd learnt from him, she expressed her disagreement with his ideas on it. It was becoming increasingly difficult for me to reconcile the musical differences between them. Rukmini paati was more orthodox in her aesthetics, and I was totally blown away by KSK maama's modernity and the way he blended it with his traditional background. Gradually, I put some distance between my grandaunt and me, citing my CA exams.

Recognising what was needed, she took the graceful approach. Rukmini paati visited me at home. 'Look, I am not able to teach you anymore. I will take you to him, he will know what to do,' she said, and formally took me to KSK maama's house. 'You should take care of him from now on,' she said to my closest friend's father, my new guru. In hindsight, I can see how beautifully she handled the situation. She knew I was getting out of hand, she was old and she truly respected KSK maama. He had a good name, even if he wasn't a 'big' name, was very knowledgeable and non-controversial. We got along famously. Until his passing, I was with him; he was my guru. I could go to his home any time of the day, and he would teach me any song I wanted to learn. His generosity was phenomenal. I would demand to learn things from him, and he allowed me that freedom. 'I want to learn a Tamil composition tuned in Vasantha raga in Misra chapu,' I'd only have to announce what my heart desired. He would have it ready for me to learn in a day.

Those who came before him had laid the foundations, but it was he who helped me think creatively. He would say, 'Don't try to sing Kambhoji like GNB; you sing your Kambhoji. GNB has sung and gone. What are you going to do?'

He helped me grow; so I went from thinking, 'What else is one to do with this raga, hasn't GNB done it all?' to 'GNB's glory isn't affected by my interpreting a raga in my, perhaps different, style. I can just sing what I want to.' He helped me understand many subtleties that would eventually show up in my music. This particular instance of an alapana in Andolika comes to mind. GNB was the master of this raga and he always began the alapana on the Ni. KSK once asked me 'Can't you begin with the rishabham [Ri] instead?' Isn't that a simple, elegant way to get a young person thinking, asking them questions to help them find a new creative path?

Even as I was learning from him, I listened to everybody. I was a chronic listener. Every evening I would go to a kutcheri. Back then, Madras had concerts every single day of the year. The entertainment section of the newspaper would announce at least one concert every day. I had no other interest. Cinema was usually reserved for that big Rajinikanth or Kamal Haasan release around Deepavali. I wasn't big on TV either (apart from watching cricket matches, that is). Between 1986 and '93, I heard around 150 to 200 concerts every year. This exercise in devoted listening had a very big creative influence on me, for the live experience was vastly different from the records I had heard. I was at Sastry Hall for a Papanasam Sivan Day kutcheri where T.M. Thyagarajan (TMT) was performing. To this day, I'm in awe of how he elaborated on the Charukesi raga at that concert. He slowly built the sangathis up, step by step, with a few unpredictable phrases sprinkled in that would catch me completely off guard, making me go 'Aha!' out loud.

He'd be singing quietly, then suddenly throw in one of those brilliant phrases, and gesture with his hands moving like a wave to show the note's journey, a smug smile on his face. It was a thrilling experience, and it was something you could only fully appreciate in person. As Thyagarajan finished the sangathi on a 'Ma' with that signature hand gesture, the hall spontaneously erupted in deafening applause.

Imagine, as an impressionable young performing artist, you find yourself in a grand concert like this. Even minor details like where the high point of the kutcheri is, how the audience reacts to it, how the performer responds to this reaction begin to register with you at a subconscious level. The next time you are on stage, you begin to see parallels. This time, as a performer, you can feed off that energy emanating from the audience yourself. These are the things one learnt from 'watching' concerts.

I would also go hunting for live concert recordings of kutcheris: Ramnad Krishnan, GNB, Semmangudi, Musiri, Ariyakudi, M.D. Ramanathan ... whatever record I could lay my hands on, I listened to over and over again.

After KSK maama passed away in 1999, I was on my own for three years, without a guru. Even before that, by 1998, our meetings had become scarce due to my busy schedule and his declining health. His passing was a paradox that was difficult for me to process. I remember feeling teary-eyed after more than one kutcheri, realising there was no one left for me to 'worry' about satisfying. Until then, I had always felt answerable to KSK maama.

If I took a liberty or tried something new, it had to be something he would approve of. I missed that watchful eye over me, just as I was finally 'free' to do what I wanted. Someone I looked up to, someone who inspired me, was no longer there. For about three years after that, I longed to find someone else to go to, someone to be with.

In 2002, I was in Trichy for a concert, when I met nadaswaram artist Kasim (Sheikh Chinna Moulana's grandson) with whom I used to talk a lot of music back in the day. He told me once about a letter he received, congratulating his radio programme, from the vidwan S.R.D. Vaidyanathan, and asked if I knew the man who would go on to influence me over the next decade. In the early nineties, at Thiruvaiyaru I had heard SRD perform a Thyagaraja krithi, 'Enduku Peddala', on the nadaswaram. I remember a particularly brilliant sangathi to which a man who was seeking alms on the street had responded with 'Sabash!' I'll never forget that moment. When he got off stage, musician Thanjavur Sankara Iyer asked me, 'Do you know who he is? This is Sembanarkoil!' I knew he was Mayuram S.R.D. Vaidyanathan (SRD), but didn't know that the S stood for Sembanarkoil. That was my first, fleeting meeting with him. I hadn't spoken to him for years since. Kasim was going to Chennai to meet SRD, who was recovering from an open heart surgery, and asked me to come along. 'He's a lovely man, you should meet him,' he said. Of course I went.

After the surgery, SRD had stopped playing the nadaswaram. He asked me if I would sing. I did. Kambhoji, if my memory serves me right. Then he sang. A padam in raga Athana, 'Summa Summa'.

It was so beautiful, I fell for it instantly and said to him in passing, 'I would like to learn this from you one day.'

He called me a fortnight later, and after we exchanged pleasantries, he probed most gently, most delightfully, 'Want to learn that Athana, do you? Are you coming?'

I went to him right away. I also heard him *sing* Mallari, and he taught it to me; I then sang it in a concert. This specialised compositional form was a stronghold of instrumentalists, especially nadaswaram artists, and barely any vocalists sang it until then. It was my guru SRD who made me sing it in a kutcheri.

Mallari is usually played by nadaswaram artists when deities from temples go on procession. Only nadaswaram artists would learn the form because of this temple tradition, and they usually perform it in three speeds, elaborating the Mallari in different ways, performing swaras, etc. Even today, when there's a Purappaadu (procession of the deity) in the temple on my street corner, they play the Mallari in Gambhira Nattai raga. That's how ubiquitous it is. Bharatanatyam performances have regularly featured Mallaris. In Carnatic concerts, instrumentalists were the first to perform them, especially Kunnakudi Vaidyanathan. He would perform with thavil (which is the percussion that accompanies nadaswaram), and so it was natural for him to borrow from the nadaswaram repertoire. No one was singing it though. SRD would sing Mallaris at home, because he could not play the nadaswaram after his surgery. This is how he came to teach it to me. Around the time that I was learning from him, I was his only vocalist student. As far as I know, everyone else was a nadaswara vidwan. One day he said to me, 'You sing Mallari, thambi, it will be nice!' I asked him why, he said, 'No one has done it. You do it and the world will praise you. It will be fantastic; wait and see.' I was so taken with everything he said and did, I didn't even have to think before agreeing to sing it. He taught me about eight Mallaris, and I began performing them right away, with swaram, korvai and kurappu. I also started singing Ragam Tanam Mallari (instead of Ragam Tanam Pallavi). When I sang these on stage, they were received very well.

Having these conversations with him opened up, psychologically, a space of freedom in singing for me. Is it because nadaswaram vidwans play out in the open that their minds too seem so open in terms of ideas? We perform inside auditoriums, and I fear that it has restricted our creative thinking. This freedom I was embracing showed up even in the way I thought about sound production. Until then, for me, sound production was a very minimalist affair, other than the upper octave where I sang full-throated. The ornamentation and phrasing of my music was mostly minute, almost like filigree work. But nadaswaram music is all about longer swoops. Sweeping sounds that go in slow, long curves. When I mixed these sweeps with raga singing, the soundscape itself began to change.

SRD would demonstrate to me, throwing his voice out wide, for instance, while he sang Todi raga, instead of singing it close-mouthed, or dwell on a sangathi expansively and ask, 'Why don't you sing like this?' I would come away thinking, *aha, I am going to work on this for my next concert*. He was also one to rebuke me when I went overboard. 'I asked you to do one thing, don't try forty different things. No need to do this much, thambi!' I needed his help to start, and then I would move further with those ideas. He opened up those spaces for me. In fact, he wanted to see the soundscaping that he used in his nadaswaram playing in my singing, because when he sang, people loved it. And when I employed the techniques he spoke about, I would see a reaction almost immediately from the audience. They would be amused, smiling.

Under his tutelage, I was beginning to gain confidence that I had the agency to choose what I was doing with my music. SRD helped me realise that, in art, there was no such thing as 'this can be done, or this should be done'. When you talk about art in a very broad sense, that's what everybody says: art is creativity unbound. But in a classical art form, you have grammar, then you have convention, then you draw all kinds of boundaries around your craft and

Talking to SRD during the filming of the documentary Aarar Asaipadaar

try to work within them. But at some point, those boundaries should become meaningless to you, so that you are still true to the grammar, but you are not confined to it. This is a transformative state. SRD gave me the gift of this state by pushing these ideas into my heart at a subconscious level.

There was a period when I hadn't gone to meet him in a while, so he called me and asked, 'What happened, thambi?' I explained that some commitments had held me up, and he joked: 'Amma [which is what I called his wife] asked if you had stopped coming because I had run out of things to teach you!'

She was very fond of me as well, and I used to give her my music CDs to listen to. SRD would often remark, 'Amma doesn't listen to anyone's music, she only has your CDs. Doesn't give them to me also.'

When he passed away in 2013, he left behind a many-textured empty space in my life. I missed his affectionate ways. And I wished I'd learnt so much more of the technical aspects of music from him, but that was a busy, travel-filled decade. More than anything, as I look back now, I think I enjoyed the fact that I could interact at such an advanced level with another artist.

Rilke's encounters with Cézanne's many shades of blues, and the difficulties he must have overcome to describe them in his letters to his wife, the sculptor Clara Westhoff, come to mind as I try to talk about my time with him. Just being in his company, listening to his experiences, I'd absorbed so much. It is from listening to senior artists like SRD and N. Ramani, whom I spoke to a lot as well, that one understood why someone in the past sang a keerthanam at a particular point in time, what its relevance was and should one sing it at all today, ideas like these, for instance.

Since SRD's passing, I've leant on my memories and learnings from both him and KSK maama, even as I miss the conversations I've had with them. The latter had inculcated in me a beautiful practice that has served me a great deal in the last twenty-five years. When KSK maama taught me a song, he would write down the notations, make a recording of him singing it and hand both over to me. When I eventually learnt how to read notations, he pointed me to resources and said, learn from them yourself when there is no recorded reference.

With the advent of records, the practice of learning from notations began to wane because it's easier to learn from an audio source than a written one. But the problem with that was you were stuck with the song as interpreted by the artist whose recording it was, and you would then find it difficult to break that interpretation because you were, in a sense, bound by it. But when you work with a source for which there is no audio available, you can interpret it yourself. You have to decide: shall I hold the 'ga' in this manner or that, shall I add this sangathi here or not. It's just you and that musical material in front of you; the material is showing you something the original writer of that notation intended. Over time, this exercise helps you understand the composer's mind. KSK maama taught me this profound yet basic musical lesson. He had this incredible ability to take any song and make it performance-worthy. Of course there were a number of musicians who could do it as well, but he was a specialist, he excelled at it; he just needed bare notations. And if there were no notations, KSK maama would just tune the song himself.

As long as he was alive, whenever I wanted musical material, I could go to him. Afterwards, when I wanted new material, I found referring to older audio sources tiring and monotonous. There was a redundancy in them, I could sense predictability. My search was for material that I could sing, that I could interpret. So over time, I started sourcing material the way KSK maama did. I would pore over books like he did for me, hunt for songs, write them down and notate them, and then I began performing those songs. I started with compositions where skeletal notations were available, then I began to set them up for performance, making the material sing in a sense.

In the last decade, I have also started setting songs to tune afresh. Take a raga like Narayani, in which there are two prominent Thyagaraja krithis and one Patnam Subramania Iyer keerthanam. Those belong to particular subgenres, composed by Mulakandu Telugu people from their respective eras. If I want to sing a Kannada song in Narayani or a Tamil song, I don't have a ready repertoire. But this is a beautiful raga, why should I sing only Thyagaraja in it? These thoughts propelled me, gathered strength in my mind. I came across an exceptional Akkamahadevi song in Karaharapriya. But there were so many songs in that raga, I decided to sing the poem in Narayani. What's the difference between the two ragas anyway? Narayani doesn't have gaandharam (the 'ga' note). I don't claim to be the first person to do any of this. Many artists before me have done this—T.N. Seshagopalan, Balamuralikrishna, Lalgudi Jayaraman. It's only that I have developed a deep interest in this area of music now. In Tamil especially, I didn't want my repertoire to be formulaic, which was a big driver for my research. For the Margazhi Maha Utsavam (MMU), which was a popular music programme on Jaya TV, I'd sing five to seven songs each year. I began to pick one song I'd heard someone sing, three songs that I'd learnt from notations and one that I set to tune myself. Over time, I've gained confidence in my process, and have come to intuit which tune works and which doesn't.

This has been the process of learning for me as a practising artist. Right now, musically, this is what I do most.

During the pandemic, I also rediscovered Balamuralikrishna. For too long, I'd ignored studying him. Going back to his music this time around was a revelation. There's so much that is unexplored, so much that he has sung that no one else has taken forward.

There was, of course, a lot of opposition to his experiments with music. That might have discouraged others. But when I listened to his ideas, they seemed so fresh to me. Ultimately, for me, it only matters that the material that I work with, that I sing, is fresh. It should be good, it shouldn't feel tiring. I enjoy learning songs from any source in front of me, that has been my nature. Balamurali's material has me hooked these days.

Even as I enjoy teaching myself constantly, I cannot say the same for how I feel about teaching others. I did it for nearly twenty-five years. But I seem to have run out of patience, no doubt the most important of virtues in a teacher. I also realised that if I listened to a student sing and commented on every aspect of their music, they were in the danger of becoming my clones. I noticed that some students tended to emulate me too closely. To be fair, I too sang like my gurus, but few have heard them sing. I am currently a practising artist, so I did not see the point of someone else singing exactly like me. Once my students began performing professionally, the feedback made me want to take a step back. These questions about pedagogy bothered me to such an extent that I decided to quit.

When I was learning, I had limited access and needed constant guidance. Today, you can learn a million things at home. You need, at best, half an hour a week with somebody to see if you're on the right track. Music classes, where you sit down and learn songs by rote may make for good social activities when you are children, but at the level of performers and professionals, there's no need for that. If I were to continue to teach today, the only reason might be the money I could make from it, but then I have never made money from teaching. I never paid my gurus; I didn't take money from my students.

It is an important income stream for musicians, and I am far from opposed to it. Especially at a time when the place for top artists is shrinking, teaching has become a big source of income for many musicians. It's only fair. But I think of myself as a performer, not a teacher. And I do hope there comes a day when there's some distinction between those who teach and those who perform.

Performers need time to think about how to bring people into the halls. Teaching eats into one's time as a serious practitioner, the time one could have spent thinking about the craft.

At thirty-five, two decades ago, I was constantly on the road for concerts. With just a day or two at home, the very idea of teaching felt burdensome. I had little time for my own art and for my children who were younger then and needed me. When I was teaching a lot, it affected my performance too. I couldn't change my lifestyle either; I had EMIs to think about. As teaching began to eat into my professional and personal time, slowly I began to give it up and turned towards a life dedicated to performance. It was also a necessary act of self-preservation, for I was going through a phase of feeling saturated, as if I was getting repetitive.

CHAPTER 3

Tamil and I

To break free from the creative rut that I found myself in, I sought inspiration from outside Carnatic music. I listened to ghazals, Hindi film music, Pakistani music, blues and jazz. I was still on the lookout for something that could find its way into my music and invigorate it when the writer Charukesi asked me to perform a concert for the Devan Memorial Trust. After my kutcheri, he gave me a set of novels by the Tamil writer Devan, celebrated for his 'Thuppariyum Sambu' detective series. This gift brought me back to Tamil fiction; after years I found myself reading in my mother tongue. These books piqued my interest and I began reading Tamil fiction more seriously.

Back in 2006, Prasanna Ramaswamy had made a film about me, *Aarar Asaippadar* (*Desired Melody*), named after a Tamil song by the sixteenth-century composer Muthu Thandavar. That brought another significant long-term creative relationship into my life. I'd known her for longer though—since 1991, when she wrote an article about my music, titled 'Oasis in a Desert', for the *Economic Times*. At that time, I was just twenty-three years old, and she had attended eight of my concerts during the afternoons. Although she

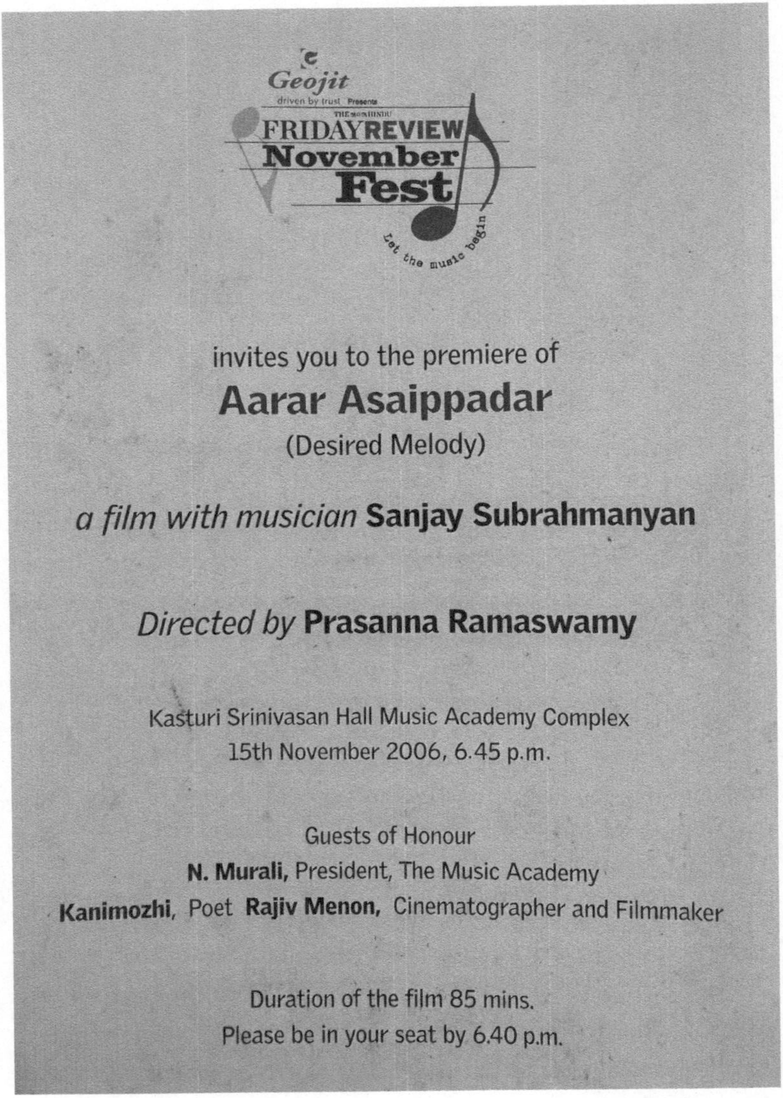

Geojit
driven by trust Presents
THE HINDU
FRIDAY REVIEW
November
Fest
Let the music begin

invites you to the premiere of

Aarar Asaippadar

(Desired Melody)

a film with musician **Sanjay Subrahmanyan**

Directed by **Prasanna Ramaswamy**

Kasturi Srinivasan Hall Music Academy Complex
15th November 2006, 6.45 p.m.

Guests of Honour
N. Murali, President, The Music Academy
Kanimozhi, Poet **Rajiv Menon,** Cinematographer and Filmmaker

Duration of the film 85 mins.
Please be in your seat by 6.40 p.m.

Aarar Asaippadar *opened at* The Hindu*'s November Fest in 2006* didn't know who I was initially, she liked my performances enough to write about me.

Later, when I got married, Prasanna reached out to me, introduced herself and expressed a desire to meet me and my wife. She was working as a programming officer at the Max Mueller Bhavan back then. A playwright, an intellectual and an artist herself, Prasanna spoke warmly about several aspects of my performance. However, she recalled a particular concert organised by Kartik Fine Arts in Bharatiya Vidya Bhavan in December 1992, where she observed something strange.

T.N. Seshagopalan had come to that afternoon's concert. The hall was packed. I wanted to make this man nod and approve of my singing. That was my only objective. I just had to. But he was just sitting there, stone-like, through the entire concert. Back then, seniors felt that you mustn't encourage younger 'boys'. I sang Athana raga and dug deeper and deeper, but that nod that I sought just never came. I went home and called Aarthi, whom I was going out with at that time, and cried. 'Wouldn't his seniors have appreciated his singing? Why did this man not even nod once?' To be fair, when I met him at his home a few weeks later, he was very warm and welcoming. He was also the first person to tell me to give up my CA career if I wanted to be a full-time musician. He insisted that having two professions did not make sense. Later when I was singing more regularly, he attended a few of my concerts, called me and offered both compliments and suggestions. When I received the Sangita Kalanidhi, he was one of the first musicians to call me.

In that very same kutcheri, where I had dug into that Athana, I'd sung 'Eti Janmamidi' in Varali raga, which Prasanna had loved and had written about in her piece for *ET*. But when she spoke to me about that concert later, she said: 'I heard you in Bharatiya Vidya Bhavan when you sang Athana. That day I thought we had lost you. I thought you were just another performing monkey. *What a loss of an artist,* I said to myself. I felt bad for two days. *What a waste of a talent,* I thought. Luckily, in the next concert nothing I feared happened.'

I told her, 'I know exactly what happened that day.' Until she explained to me how she felt that day, I'd never thought about what I might have sounded like to the audience when I was angling for Seshagopalan's nod!

Over the years, we developed a warm friendship, and in 2004, she came up with the idea of a film. I was only thirty-five then. I said to her, 'A documentary already?' She said, 'Fine, don't call it a documentary, let's say I want to make a film with you.' I agreed. We still have about twenty-eight hours of footage from that film, which she edited to a 110-minute film. The documentary opened up a new space for me among the Tamil cultural intelligentsia, and I found myself drawn further into this exciting milieu in 2005 when I participated in an extensive interview with *Kalachuvadu* magazine. The interview, conducted again by Prasanna, along with documentary filmmaker R.V. Ramani and writer Yuvan Chandrashekar (with whom I love discussing Tamil literature), lasted fifteen hours and explored my musical journey in-depth. It was *Kalachuvadu*'s practice to have their interviewers engage for long hours with interviewees. Every time I said something, one of them would have a question, and the conversation would travel in a new direction. They were looking for something, not even they knew what, and until we were satisfied with an answer, we would keep talking. The photo that accompanied the interview was shot by Puduvai Ilavenil, featuring me in my moustache-and-long-hair look of those days. This interview garnered significant attention among Tamil intellectuals, and introduced me to a wider audience. It was after this that I made a lot of writer friends. Until then, Tamil to me meant only Gopalakrishna Bharathi, Papanasam Sivan and some songs from KSK maama's Tamil repertoire from his Annamalai University days. These pieces were musically significant, focusing on a new raga or a fresh aesthetic angle to a composition. But my focus until then was never on the language or content, but purely on the music itself.

When I started reading and exploring this whole new world outside Mylapore and Madras, that began influencing how I wrote pallavis, how I sang songs. I began to think differently about lyrics in pallavis, digging deeper for compositions. It is from this milieu and the exposure I got from it that I ended up working with the Tamil language so much. Over the next six years, I immersed myself in Tamil literature. I met more and more writers, who also recommended pallavis and poems that I could adapt for my concerts.

I was not yet forty and bursting with creative energy, exploring and absorbing these influences. Everywhere I went, I found inspiration; I enjoyed scouting for unique songs. Like the accidental discovery of a cassette with Viswanatha Iyer's music in my father's house, which led me to learn and perform the song 'Parengum Parthaalum' in Kalyani raga in a few concerts, including one in Kumbakonam, because of the line 'Kumbakona kshetram tanile' (In the holy town of Kumbakonam) in the song. Those who heard the concert in Kumbakonam were expectedly very pleased. As my interest in Tamil grew, I found my musical repertoire expanding, prompting colleagues and audiences to wonder about my sources. All this was before YouTube existed. Now there is so much more material readily available for us to explore.

In the beginning of my career too I sang Tamil songs, but for very different reasons. In the eighties, D.K. Jayaraman (DKJ) was a big musical star, and Rukmini paati was a fan. She admired how adept he was at handling Tamil compositions. I still remember a radio special of his from the early eighties; he sang the prolific Papanasam Sivan's compositions for the entirety of the performance, including a moving 'Tamasama Amma' in Kuntalavarali. I religiously attended his concerts in Chennai after that—they were such a delight, particularly because he sang Tamil songs with conviction and emotion. DKJ was my grandaunt's initial inspiration for introducing Tamil compositions to my repertoire. She helped me learn songs like 'Unnaiyallaal' in Kalyani and 'Enadumanam' in Harikambhoji from his recordings. In those early years, his influence on my music was so strong that even some musicians, like K.V. Narayanaswamy (KVN), mistakenly believed that I was Jayaraman's disciple. During the Festember music competition in REC Trichy, where KVN was a judge announcing the result, he said that, even as he heard me sing, he knew I was DKJ's disciple. Of course, I immediately clarified that I wasn't. Another time, after I had finished recording a radio programme, A.P. Komala, the tambura artist, asked if I was his student.

Even before DKJ's concert, I'd heard Papanasam Sivan's work. His family and disciples sang them during the margazhi month, walking through the lanes of Mylapore's Kapaleeshwarar temple, doing bhajan sessions. I still remember, in the mid-eighties, one day Thyagu thaatha came home very excited. He had just visited his good old friend Neelu (Neelakantan who was the son of violin vidwan Thiruvalangadu Sundaresa Iyer) and had heard someone sing. That artist's name was Balu, and he was a disciple of Papanasam Sivan. Thaatha was raving non-stop about the bhaavam, the intensity and the creativity of his singing, especially viruthams. This was my introduction to the music of Sethalapathy Balasubramaniam. My grandfather came back home that day and immediately contacted Balu maama and asked him to come home and sing for all of us. He felt that the void created by the loss of GNB to the musical world had finally been filled.

Balu maama arrived with his son and mridangam artist Ganapathyraman and sang for about an hour and a half. It was a very new experience for us. We were immediately hooked to his uninhibited, emotive style of singing. And that margazhi, we began attending his Sivan bhajanai sessions on the streets around the Kapaleeswarar temple. Every morning, my parents and I would be up by 5.30 to listen to his bhajanai. Balu maama was a cult figure in those days. There was a group of about fifteen to twenty people who were devoted listeners of his music, and we joined that loyal band of fanatics.

A few others also sang bhajans. Prominent among them was Balu maama's uncle Mani Bhagavatar, who unfortunately passed away within a year or so after we started attending these sessions. Mani Bhagavatar was a giant of a singer; a small, frail-looking man, but with a singing voice of four kattai (F scale) shruthi and big volume. He sounded to me a bit like the old Musiri Subramania Iyer of the 78-rpm-record days. He sang some interesting songs like 'Amba Manam Kaninthu' in Pantuvarali (made famous by M.K. Thyagaraja Bhagavathar, or MKT),'Marundalitthiduvaai' in Gowla and one of his specials, 'Kaadali Raadhayai' in Kharaharapriya, which reduced Aruna Sairam to uncontrollable tears once.

Then there was Rukmini Ramani, Papanasam Sivan's daughter, and a few disciples of hers, and her son, the talented Papanasam Ashok Ramani. The popular star there was, however, Balu maama.

A few days into margazhi, the requests would start pouring in for him to sing. His favourites were Todi, Kambhoji, Kharaharapriya and Shanmukhapriya. He also loved singing Mohanam, Hindolam, Kapi, Sindhu Bhairavi, Behag and Suddha Dhanyasi. I was a huge fan of several of his trademark viruthams, which is basically improv singing of poetry, like 'Oorilen Kaani', 'Maarinindru Ennai' and 'Ullaasa Nirakula'. Some days Lalgudi Swaminatha Odhuvar, the resident singer of the Kapaleeswarar temple, would join in, and the two would launch into a virutham jugalbandhi. Whatever else they sang, Keeravani and Kapi ragas were mandatory.

For me, Balu maama was like a manasika guru, the teacher I never trained under. I loved the way he articulated lyrics when singing viruthams, especially dwelling on specific words and enhancing them with a torrent of sangathis. He was a huge fan of Madurai Mani Iyer and GNB. Balu maama came to my wedding and blessed Aarthi and me with a spontaneous virutham; it was the best gift a student could receive. We began collecting some of his records, and one such recording I treasure is his concert at the residence of the actor-musician Kothamangalam Seenu. I got this recording from Seenu's son, Ganesh, who was my regular tambura artist. Unfortunately, the quality of Meltrack cassettes were so bad that the recording is now lost to me.

S.V. Krishnan (SVK), who ran the concert venue Ragasudha Hall, too liked Balu maama's music a lot and frequently invited him to his house to sing. On one such occasion, I was playing the tambura. There was an old friend of SVK's, an amateur mridangam artist, who was playing for him. Balu maama was really irritated with his playing, and after a couple of songs he called out to mridangist Arun Prakash, who was sitting in the audience, and said, 'Antha kozhantha rendu paattukku vaasikkattum.' *Let that child play for a couple of songs.*

The bhajanai also attracted a lot of vidwans on a regular basis. S. Ramanathan often came and would invariably sing 'Kumaran Taal' in Yadukulakambhoji or 'Aarukkuthaan Theriyum' in Devamanohari. He would then request Mani Bhagavatar to specifically sing 'Paraamukham Yenayya' in Kharaharapriya. D.K. Jayaraman too joined these sessions on the New Year's morning.

I think Rukmini paati brought me into her vast world of Tamil songs because she felt they might give me an edge in competitions.

She made sure to teach me all her personal favourites. I learnt of the breadth of her Tamil repertoire from the sheer number of songs she bequeathed to me: Sivan's 'Sivakamasundari' in Mukhaari, 'Kandaa Vandarul' in Aabheri, 'Aadum Deivam' in Kambhoji, 'Kamala Padamalar' in Harikambhoji, 'Karthikeya' and 'Kadaikkan Nokki' in Todi, 'Attharunam Abhayam' in Bhairavi, Nila Ramamurti's ragamalika 'Maasil Ayodiyil', Bharatiyar's 'Solla Vallaayo', a ragamalika, Gopalakrishna Bharati's 'Satre Vilagi' in Poorvikalyani, 'Vazhi Maraittirukkude' in Nattakurinji, Ramanatakam songs like 'Annai Janaki', 'Ramanukku Mannan' and 'Arivaar Yaar'. She also taught me Tamil padams like Ghanam Krishna Aiyyar's 'Yaar Poi Solluvaar' in Todi, Duraiswamy Kavirayar's 'Innum Paramukham Eno' in Begada, Ghanam Krishna Iyer's 'Niddiraiyil' and Koteeswara Iyer compositions like 'Ayyane Aatkol' and 'Velava' in Keeravani.

When I learnt these songs in the eighties, I had focused on their musical aspects—ragas, phrases and sangathis. I never paid attention to the words, and my grandaunt rarely delved into the text's meaning. Instead, she focused on giving me small, impactful suggestions, such as musical modulations that made emotions come through. Her insights, even then, had helped me deliver the text in a refined manner onstage. Before every kutcheri, she made sure to ask me what Tamil song I had in mind. Even in my first appearance at the 12 o'clock slot at the Music Academy in 1989, I sang the Tamil song 'Aadum Deivam' in Kambhoji as the main piece. She felt strongly that the local language accessible to everyone had to feature. I did get the sense that she was heavily influenced by the Tamil Isai Movement, which sought to propagate Tamil compositions and composers in Carnatic music, and M.S. Subbulakshmi, one of her icons. She even modelled her singing after MS, one of the first proponents of Tamil songs in sabhas. My grandaunt never explicitly discussed the politics of it all with me, however. I knew that she also learnt a vast number of Tamil compositions directly from Koteeswara Iyer and Papanasam Sivan. She had also learnt some majestic padams in Tamil from T. Brinda.

It so happened that KSK maama also shared this love for Tamil. Around 1941–42, he was in Annamalai University, which was the seat of the Tamil Isai Movement. He often recalled his university days, about the gurukulam-like atmosphere that prevailed there, and how the teachers insisted that students wake up early in the morning to practice. Through my decade with him, I learnt Tamil songs from his extensive repertoire.

He taught me an entire album's worth of Koteeswara Iyer songs, which I went on to record in 1990. After that, my musical interests shifted towards other material. We would occasionally sing 'tukdas' together, some Subramania Bharati songs that he had set to tune, like 'Pagaivanukkarulvai', 'Kaani Nilam' and 'Ethanai Kodi'. He liked to hum these for me as well, though I wasn't as enamoured of them. Back then, my musical instincts were classical and a tad puritanical. Even some of KSK maama's tunes were too modern for my taste. With time though, my preferences have evolved.

How I came to perform the now-famous Tamil song 'Kaalai Thooki' for the first time is amusing to me even now. My Malaysian friend Jega once mentioned a friend of his named Thiru, who had a New Year's tradition of getting drunk and breaking into the famous dance pose from the song 'Kaalai Thooki'. It is a classical song about Nataraja's pose. He casually referred to it as the 'Kaalai Thooki dance', but I had never heard of such a song. Back then, it wasn't particularly popular, and I hadn't come across any earlier recordings by the masters. Curious, I asked KSK maama about it, and he taught it to me right away. I liked it so much that I performed it at the Academy for that year's season (1992-93), where it was received very well. It was only then that I realised how

Kaalai thookki

6/27/23 6:16 PM

27-06-2023 18:21
A song about how I learnt Kaalai thookki

Jega narrated a story about his friend
Every year on New Year's Eve
He would get drunk and do the Kaalai thooki dance

I asked him what was Kaalai thookki
He told me it was a popular song
I asked my teacher about this
He sang and showed me the first line
I had to learn it immediately

It was at the Music Academy
I sang Kaalai thookki
People forgot the concert
But remembered Kaalai thookki

A song that jogged people's memory
A song that reminded them of MS Subbulakshmi
A song that spoke of the cosmic dance
A song that got revived from a drunken friend's dance

Kaalai thookki

காலைத் தூக்கி நின்றாடும் தெய்வமே

நண்பர் ஜகா சொன்ன கதை
நியூயர் பார்ட்டியில் நடந்த கதை
ஒருவர் குடித்து ஆடிய ஆட்டம்
அந்த ஆட்டத்திற்கு பாடிய பாட்டு
காலைத் தூக்கி நின்றாடும் தெய்வமே

அறியாத பாட்டாதலால் குருவிடம் கேட்டேன்
முதல் வரியைப் பாடினார் மனம் குளிர்ந்தேன்
பாட வேண்டுமென்று முடிவு செய்தேன்
உடனே பாடமும் பண்ணினேன்
காலைத் தூக்கி நின்றாடும் தெய்வமே

3rd Feb 2024

ஆக்காடமியில் பாடிய ஒரு கச்சேரி
அன்று பாடிய ஒரு பாட்டு
காலைத் தூக்கி நின்றாடும் தெய்வமே
ரசிகர் க்ச்சேரியை மறந்தாரோ
ஆனால் மறக்காமலிருந்தது
காலைத் தூக்கி நின்றாடும் தெய்வமே

ரசிகர் மனதில் நின்ற ஒரு பாட்டு
சுப்புலக்ஷ்மியை நினைவுபடுத்திய ஒரு பாட்டு
சிவனின் ஆட்டமோ குடித்த நண்பனின் ஆட்டமோ
நினைவில் நின்றது
காலைத் தூக்கி நின்றாடும் தெய்வமே

Sourcing new material looked a little different before the Internet beloved M.S. Subbulakshmi's version was among older audiences; they instantly recognised it.

After KSK maama was gone, I revisited the Subramania Bharati songs, and it was a completely different experience this time. There still remains a wealth of material he gave me on Bharati that I am yet to explore. Only recently did I truly discover the song 'Nitham Unnai' in the raga Chakravakam, even though I have decades-old recordings of him teaching me this composition.

The launch of Margazhi Maha Utsavam, the televised Carnatic music programme produced by Subhashree Thanikachalam, was a turning point in the development of my Tamil repertoire. In 2003, Subhashree suggested I sing a concert featuring only Bharati's songs. I set 'Chandiran Oliyil' to tune in Malayamarutham and tuned 'Vande Mataram' in Kedaram. Both these songs ended up becoming regular features in my concerts.

For a decade that followed, I found myself drawn to Tamil composers, and songs known and unknown. In 2005, for instance, I was immersed in volumes of Papanasam Sivan's compositions. This is when I stumbled upon his song 'Karpagambigai' on the goddess of Mylapore in Behag raga. Until then, I'd never strictly adhered to original notations. I treated them as foundations upon which to build my interpretations, at times even deviating from them. But while learning this song, I made an effort to stay true to the notations. This process unveiled to me Sivan's musical genius. It broadened my vision of the raga, and added to my knowledge of ideas and phrases that would go on to resurface in my art in different ways when I was performing or composing. The work I did on this song also marked a shift in my approach to learning new songs. Previously, I would learn a song, sing it and hardly revisit it. But I dedicated a week or more to singing and working with the Behag, and this method has stayed with me since. Looking back, I can't quite believe what I was doing in the late nineties—learning a Navavarnam in the afternoon and performing it that evening in a concert and forgetting it the next day!

My MMU concert theme for the following year, 2006, marked another turning point in my journey with the language. It took me forward in ways I hadn't imagined then. That July, mridangam exponent (Guruvayur) Dorai maama performed an informal housewarming concert in our home. The way he sang the arutpa 'Appa Naan', about showing love to all things living, in Purvikalyani raga moved me so deeply that I instantly wanted to make it my own at concerts. And with this began my search for arutpas—there were 5,818 of them, composed by Ramalingaswamy or Vallalar, a nineteenth-century saint-poet who advocated compassion and eschewed caste-based discrimination.

Years later, I was once again moved by another gesture because of this very song. The renowned Tamil writer Perumal Murugan took me by surprise, with a mention and a thanks in the foreword to the sequel to his *Madhorubagan*. He wrote that he heard my music, and specifically this song, during the writing of the novel. The song seemed to hold some sway over him just as it had over me.

Back in 2006, when I stumbled upon a collection of arutpa recordings by Dorai maama's sister, Guruvayur Ponnammal, I decided to sing them for my MMU concert. That was the first time I broke free from my own very conventional outlook towards Tamil and Tamil compositions. But for the occasional song here and there, Ramalingaswamy had not made it to mainstream Carnatic music concerts until then. Performing these songs wasn't much of a challenge musically. Dorai maama himself gave me a copy of Ponnamal's arutpa notations. I also fondly remember learning the song 'Idu Nalla Tharunam' from my guru, SRD, for that concert.

Over the next few years, unearthing a number of little-known Tamil compositions for these televised concerts became a serious project for me. They also gave me the perfect opportunity to curate a list of theme-based songs. There had always been this 'criticism' that Tamil compositions were not heavy or classical enough to be included in mainstream concerts. I used my concerts to specifically focus on composers and compositions that invalidated this claim. Discovering a brilliant Tamil swaraakshara swarajati in Todi ragam by Mayuram Viswanatha Sastri, for instance, made me feel like a kid in a candy shop. (Sastri most famously composed Jayati Jayati Bharata Mata among many other Bharat bhajans, patriotic songs, right after Independence.) Dandapani Desigar's 'Adiyenai' in Kambhoji raga too comes to mind now as I think of the many classically heavy Tamil songs I've sung. From the works of the Tamil Moovar or trinity (Muthu Thandavar, Arunachala Kavi and Marimutha Pillai) to Harikesanallur Muthaiah Bhagavathar, the Bharathi Moovar (Kavi Kunjara Bharathi, Mazhavai Chidambara Bharathi and Suddhananda Bharathi), Duraiswami Kavirayar and Ramaswamy Sivan—the material I got to work with for this project was seemingly endless.

The extensive reach of television allowed many people to listen, and to subsequently request some of these songs in live concerts and recordings. This ensured that the compositions didn't fade away after a single performance, and that they continued to stay relevant to me. This is how Bharatidasan's 'Tunbam Nergayil' set to tune in Desh raga by Dandapani Desigar became one of the most requested songs in my concerts for years. It was also the first song on my YouTube channel to hit a million views.

I first heard the song in the late eighties, when my love for Desh was at its peak. I was loath to sing it in kutcheris then because it had appeared in a film. I didn't know much else about the song back then. As my own musical sense, aesthetics and priorities evolved, in 2008, I sang this song for the first time on Desigar's birth centenary.

KSK maama always held Desigar in high regard for his musicality. He introduced me to songs like 'Unnai Andri' in Bhavani, 'Arulvaai Angayarkanni' in Dharmavati and 'Ennai Nee Maravade' in Amrutavarshini ragam. It was from my guru's copy of Desigar compositions that I learnt ragas like Tandavam from the song 'Kadavulai Maravade', which I now regularly sing in ragamalika swarams. Years ago, I heard a superb rendition of a song, 'Narayananai Thuthipaai', set to tune by Desigar in the Komalangi raga, at a concert by 'TAFE' Mahadevan. (As an aside, his grandson, cricketer Abhinav Mukund, opened batting for Tamil Nadu and India in the Ranji trophy and was in the Chennai Super Kings and the Royal Challengers Bangalore.) After I heard that song, I began singing 'Komalangi' in viruthams and ragamalika swarams as well.

In 2008, as I perused Desigar's sixty-odd compositions and the fifty other songs he set to tune, it was evident to me that mainstream Carnatic music had missed out on a really classy vidwan. He had a firm grounding in traditional values and a rebellious mind that dwelt on the realms of the unfamiliar and novel. Today, I can only say that it's sad that Desigar has not been given his due. KSK maama always felt that it was perhaps due to the politics of his time more than anything else. He even wished Desigar hadn't been so overtly political, because neither awards nor honours from the traditional Carnatic music circles, especially the Academy and other sabhas, came his way. He associated himself with the Tamil Isai Movement and the Dravidian Movement politically, both of which alienated the so-called purists of the Carnatic music domain. The plank of the Dravidian Movement was anti-brahminism, and the sabhas were led largely by a brahmin lobby. I have even heard that when he sang a Tamil song in Thiruvaiyaru, the premises were 'purified' with water afterwards.

His contemporaries had no problem with him though. People like Lalgudi and GNB accepted and acknowledged his talent. Lalgudi has, in fact, accompanied Desigar, performed his compositions and taught them to his students. It is the ecosystem which ran the sabhas that did not acknowledge Desigar.

As KSK maama said, 'He was a brilliant musician and he set songs to tune beautifully. He knew how to make any song a hit in a kutcheri because he was a performer. In fact all songs he tuned were hits. I can't say the same for the songs I tune, they rarely become popular.' Only a handful of us performed Desigar's music, and I wanted to pay a tribute to him, which is why I decided to celebrate his material that year, and his music has since stayed with me. Vidwan P. Muthukumaraswamy, also the father of renowned visual artist Padmavasan and a disciple of Desigar and KSK, helped me with the concert. Not only did he give me a few songs, he also came to the concert and spoke with great warmth and appreciation about the fact that a great man's birth centenary was being celebrated thus.

A few years later, around 2013, I listened to a programme of Divya Prabandha Isai, a collection of pasurams (verses) on Vishnu by the twelve bhakti saint-poets, Azhwars. Isai Perarignar Late Kanchipuram M.N. Venkatavaradhan, who was one of the stalwarts of the genre had performed them. As soon I heard it, I decided that I wanted to sing some verses too. He had set to music hundreds of pasurams, and sang them with much verve and passion well into his eighties. My good friend Yessel Narasimhan helped source written notations of several Azhwar pasurams as tuned by Venkatavaradhan himself. I was stunned by the musical and aesthetic value of his contribution to the Divya Prabandha Isai. He had set them to music in mostly traditional ragas incorporating many conventional phrases and graces. One could see a passionate soul at work in the way the sangathis had been introduced into the pasurams at appropriate places, keeping in mind the lyrical beauty and devotion of the Azhwars' works. Again, it is unfortunate that his contribution went largely unnoticed and unrecognised by the mainstream Carnatic music world, but thankfully, organisations like the Tamizh Isai Sangam gave him his due.

For my own grandaunt Rukmini Rajagopalan's birth centenary, I sang an exclusive concert of Tamil padams in 2014. She'd sung one such concert herself thirty-five years earlier, and I even remembered her superb song list: 'Innum Paraamukham' in Begada, 'Yaar Poi Solvar' in Todi, 'Nitthirayil' in Pantuvarali, 'Ethanai Sonnaalum' in Saveri and 'Velavare' in Bhairavi. The Tamil padam is a compositional form deeply rooted in Bharatanatyam, as well as the Carnatic concert tradition, for over 150 years. In the twentieth century, it displayed three main characteristics: the lyrics portrayed sringara rasa primarily, where the nayaka might either be the Lord himself or a maharaja or even a wealthy patron. The songs were basically in what are traditionally defined as 'rakti' ragas (associated with more ancient melodies and even folk music); the song was generally slow. In Carnatic music concerts, padams were sung mostly as 'miscellaneous' components, after the RTP. These compositions, I've always believed, are beautiful and have enough scope to be sung anywhere in the concert format. The one in my grandaunt's memory, where I put these notions to test, singing only padams, was proof that my belief wasn't misplaced.

While the nineteenth-century composer Samuel Vedanayagam Pillai's words have found a place of prominence in several Carnatic musicians' concerts, in the December of 2016, I found it particularly fulfilling to set to music and sing his quirky 'Paname' for my MMU concert that year. That song about the fickle nature of money from over a hundred years ago, seemed to have taken on a new meaning and relevance in the aftermath of the year's demonetisation. Alathur Venkatesa Iyer had originally tuned it in Shankarabharanam. I'd settled on Mand raga for it, it was the lightest and closest to the original raga.

These regular Tamil concerts also gave me a chance to learn new forms within the Carnatic tradition. The DMK leader Durai Murugan would often request a kaavadi chindu, a folk form that features in Carnatic music and Bharatanatyam performances, and is usually in praise of Lord Murugan. I'd always come away feeling sheepish because I hadn't learnt a single piece in the genre. Once, as I was looking through the musicologist-singer S. Ramanathan's notations for kavadi chindus, I found a song by Annamalai Reddiyar, 'Seervalar Pasunthogai Mayilan', in two different versions. The experience of combining the two versions into a double ragamalika, changing the tempo to add some variety and singing it was thoroughly enjoyable. It has since become a regular in my concert list.

Even as each of these efforts helped me fall in love with the Tamil language more, I'd all along felt a sense of guilt that many of the pieces I sang over that decade had not been repeated. A few did make it to my concerts elsewhere, but there were always so many newer songs to learn, tune and sing. All of this seemed to have been building up to my Tamizhum Naanum series of concerts, where I performed only Tamil songs for the entire three hours. Every year since 2018, I have stepped up to produce my own show, going rogue, if only slightly, by not waiting for that call to come to me in order to make a concert happen, as is the norm. Ever since I was a young performer, I was adamant about not calling someone about a concert—that felt almost like an insult to my self-esteem. Now I have now started to perform this Tamil-only concert abroad as well, using an event manager to help run my own show. Stand-up comedian Aravind S.A., who attended one of my margazhi concerts for the Tamil Isai Sangam, mooted the idea of a well-produced and, most importantly, self-produced concert. It has now taken a life of its own over the last six years.

My aunt Usha is also an advertising and branding professional. She strategised and brought Tamizhum Naanum to fruition when I approached her for advice on producing a show in 2018.

To be honest, when I finally decided to venture outside the 'system' to create a show like Tamizhum Naanum, it was as a reaction to the fact that I had been singing in the Margazhi Maha Utsavam series for some part of the eighteen years without satisfaction. I felt I was not being valued, even financially, despite putting in such an immense effort for years. Unearthing compositions, setting them to tune, learning these ancient verses and singing them in a concert all take time and effort. Now, with this series, I feel that I have an audience that respects this effort. This is a cultural shift, both for me and the audience, and it's also part of a larger idea I have for my own music. My interest in Tamil music has been taking me in newer directions, and I am vastly excited about where it's going next.

While singing in Tamil is a personal passion, I do not intend to abandon my core repertoire. After all, my early training immersed me in the works of the Carnatic Trinity, and their music has shaped me into the musician I am today. My other project, Sanjay Sabha Live, features self-produced Carnatic music kutcheris, and mirrors concerts that I continue to perform in sabhas and traditional venues. The repertoire here spans multiple languages, featuring compositions by the Trinity and other great composers.

Initially, the music season itself was very small in terms of scale. As I've said before, I too grew with the season. When I was a little boy, there were only four or five sabhas, and so the whole season's schedule would appear in just one page. Now there are entire supplements dedicated to the season.

Vani Mahal, Krishna Gana Sabha, Mylapore Fine Arts, Music Academy and Tamil Isai Sangam were the only sabhas back then. There used to be concerts in Sastry Hall, but they never hosted a festival of their own during the season. By the time I started singing, the season had begun to grow. In a way, I was in it all the time. The season was celebrated in our homes. It was like a festival for a fortnight, from 15 December to 1 January, after which things would dial down. But during that fortnight, our days were full of concerts. If I had a concert, I would finish mine and go and listen to others. After the children were born, I went alone, while Aarthi stayed at home. Sometimes we would leave our children with her parents or mine and go together. I heard almost everybody who was performing regularly until the early 2000s.

Once I became slightly better known, people started conversing with me, and it became difficult to listen to the concerts. While I used to like sitting in the back rows sometimes, it became intrusive to both me as well as the artist performing. Gradually, I had to give up on my regular concert attendance. Most musicians of my own generation and a few from the one immediately after regularly attended each other's concerts. But once professional rivalries set in, you skip some people's concerts; you'd rather go to show solidarity to someone else. I did make an effort to attend the concerts of older musicians. They were all very affectionate to me. Every time I finished singing at a concert, I would run into some of the elders at the venue, and they'd each call out to me, speak with me, take ownership of me and share stories. Attending concerts was also a PR exercise for all of us artists. We were seen, we spoke to people, all this was important; we worked with and for the system. I was very much a part of the season in every way until the pandemic, even if I had to cut down on performing for some sabhas.

Over time, I have come to believe that unrestricted growth isn't in the best interest of the art form or the artists. I'm not completely convinced that enough people are coming out and listening to concerts anymore. From five sabhas to about fifty sabhas now, each featuring eight concerts a day, what's the audience like, you ask? The attendance in many concerts stands at ten to fifteen people at best. It doesn't make sense at all. One wonders why money is being spent like this. This one time, I went to a sabha and found that there were more performers than audience members. That's heartbreaking for the artists. One of the reasons, perhaps, is that there is no unifying body to decide how to take the season forward with a vision. Usually, a festival or cultural activity has a head that issues guidelines, so that the greatest number of people may benefit. But such was not the case here.

At one point I was singing at twenty concerts, but making very little. Not all twenty concerts were house-full either. So, I slowly started identifying the ones that no longer worked for me because of one of these two reasons. I was down to twelve season concerts just before COVID. After the pandemic, I have further reduced the number to five or six. I still sing those big concerts, but now I am using the rest of the time to produce my own shows, like Tamizhum Naanum or Sanjay Sabha Live, which is satisfying in a number of ways.

It is also a fact that some sabhas, or those who control them, have not exactly been wholly accepting of my success. At fifty, after having reached a level of success, I feel justified in demanding that I be paid a certain amount. However, there are people older than me, more experienced and willing to perform for less. So the sabhas ask, 'Why should we pay you more?' For them it's almost an ego issue. In fact, some sabhas decided among themselves not to pay the amount I demanded when I first started quoting my own pay.

All said and done though, the season still works because there are spaces that draw a big crowd, and people still look forward to being there. It's also a fact that a few artists are big crowd-pullers during the season, but when they sing at other times they don't get much audience. This too makes me sad. I've always felt that satellite television brought a marked decline in live attendance for Carnatic concerts outside the season. With the advent of the internet and social media, especially YouTube, it has only worsened. People's interest in coming and listening to live events has further diminished.

Now, after the pandemic, in Chennai, other than during the music season, Carnatic festivals have nearly come to an end. Not much happens during the rest of the year, and when there is an event, there are no audiences to be had. I also think the younger generation is not into Carnatic music as much. In the eighties and nineties, we grew up in an atmosphere where this music was always with us. There was a time when there was not even a television in our homes. The internet generation has a mobile phone in its hands. They have a different way of experiencing what they want. To trigger such an audience to come and listen, we have to retune and readjust our ways. Children still learn Carnatic music. So many families from south India (and the south Indian diaspora) encourage this, and it's a good thing. These children will grow up to be the audience of tomorrow. Artists must step up their game, build their own following and draw crowds to live performances. Young musicians are smart and creative. They just need a bit of initiative and some clever marketing allies. I'm confident that, in the coming years, more people will come to live concerts even if the digital world shapes our lives.

CHAPTER 4

Radio Days

Appa was a station engineer in All India Radio Calcutta in the 1960s, and knew quite a bit about the significance of musical competitions on the radio. And because of Rukmini paati's radio career, in our family circles, it was common knowledge that, if you wanted to make your presence felt in Carnatic music, one, you needed to practise; two, you had to enter competitions; three, you had to get into All India Radio; four, you had to sing in the Thyagaraja Aaradhana.

By 1984, I had more or less given up the violin and was singing more. Right after I wrapped up class ten, my mother insisted I go sing in a radio youth programme called Ilaya Bharatham on Madras B station. The rules were simple: two songs in ten minutes. This was to be my first ever programme, and I was as inexperienced as they came. I was sixteen when I signed their contract (after reading through four pages of the most incomprehensible legalese).

A while later, I received a postcard from someone called V. Sethupathy who said he was playing the mridangam for me for the Ilaya Bharatham programme, and that it required a rehearsal. He'd said his father would also be around, and asked me to come to his home for a practice session. I made my way up to the top floor of a house near the famed Karpagambal Mess in Mylapore, where a huge photograph of a nadaswaram vidwan dominated the living room. Who had time for questions at sixteen? His father was sitting there through the rehearsal, and after we were done, he even took the time to sing the same song and offer a few pointers. Even then it didn't strike me to ask for his name or that of the vidwan in the photo. Just another music teacher, I assumed.

On the day of recording, I had a ten-minute slot from 7.40 a.m. to 7.50 a.m. I reached the station at seven and was soon joined by Sethupathy. We were allowed in only at 7.15 a.m. There wasn't going to be live tambura, just a sruti box, and I suspected no violin either. But at 7.36 a.m. sharp, who else should walk in briskly but Dwaram Mangathayaru! She sat beside us, and even as the announcement was on, she quickly tuned her violin and was ready to play. It took her just three minutes to do all of this. That was my first brush with a true professional who knew how to manage their time perfectly.

After the programme, we walked to the duty room to collect our cheques and were asked for 25 paise for a revenue stamp. I was penniless! I took an impromptu 25 paise loan from Sethupathy, and that was that. A couple of weeks later, I found myself at a concert watching Sethupathy's father perform onstage alongside Thiruvarur Sethuraman. Only then did I realise—the man whose house I had been to, my mridangist's father was the singer Kuzhikkarai Viswalingam, and the nadaswaram vidwan in the photo? The legendary Kuzhikkarai Pichayappa.

The second time I went to record for Ilaya Bharatham was in 1985. I was not yet an AIR-graded artist, but had an equally thrilling brush this time too. Another senior violinist, Kovai Dakshinamurthy, played for me. The mridangam was by a staff member of AIR, Easwaran maama. When I started singing, the

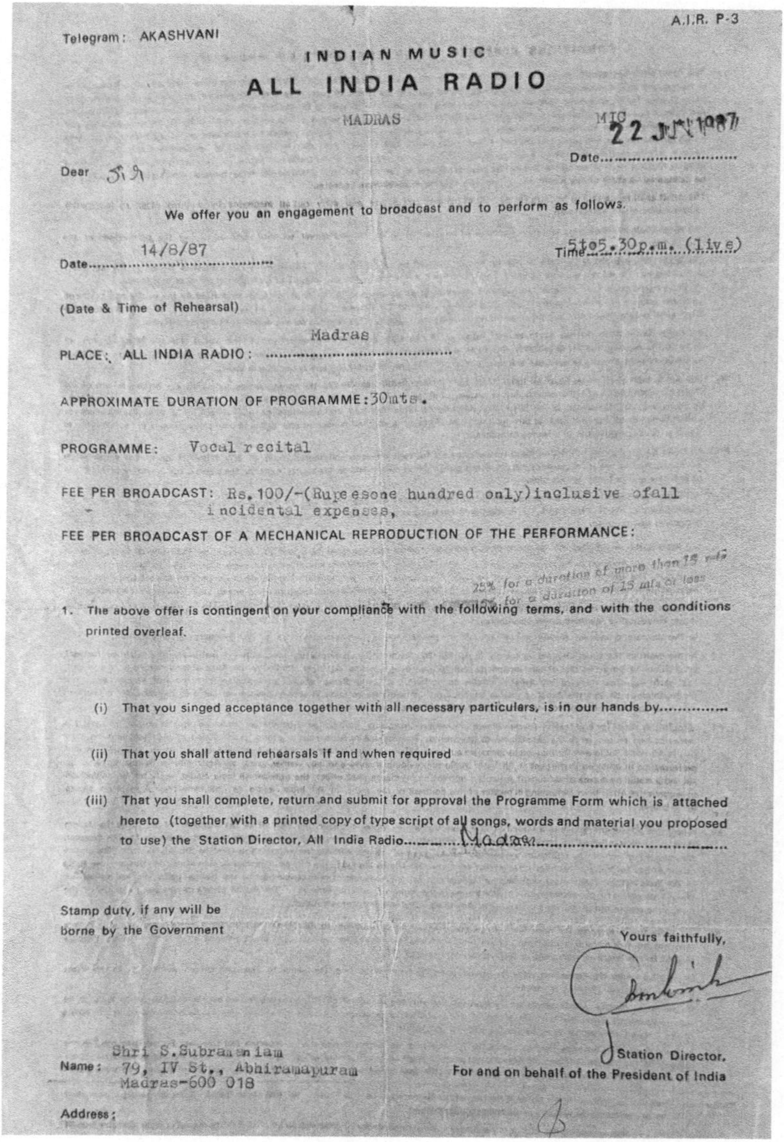

A.I.R. P-3

Telegram: AKASHVANI

INDIAN MUSIC

ALL INDIA RADIO

MADRAS

Date MIC 22 JUN 1987

Dear श्री

We offer you an engagement to broadcast and to perform as follows.

Date 14/8/87 Time 5 to 5.30 p.m. (live)

(Date & Time of Rehearsal)

PLACE: ALL INDIA RADIO: Madras

APPROXIMATE DURATION OF PROGRAMME: 30mts.

PROGRAMME: Vocal recital

FEE PER BROADCAST: Rs. 100/-(Rupees one hundred only) inclusive of all incidental expenses,

FEE PER BROADCAST OF A MECHANICAL REPRODUCTION OF THE PERFORMANCE:

25% for a duration of more than 15 mts
for a duration of 15 mts or less

1. The above offer is contingent on your compliance with the following terms, and with the conditions printed overleaf.

(i) That you singed acceptance together with all necessary particulars, is in our hands by..............

(ii) That you shall attend rehearsals if and when required

(iii) That you shall complete, return and submit for approval the Programme Form which is attached hereto (together with a printed copy of type script of all songs, words and material you proposed to use) the Station Director, All India Radio........ Madras

Stamp duty, if any will be borne by the Government

Yours faithfully,

Station Director,
For and on behalf of the President of India

Name: Shri S. Subramaniam
79, IV St., Abhiramapuram
Madras-600 018

Address:

The first contract I signed with AIR

famous mridangist and vocalist T.V. Gopalakrishnan (TVG) walked in and heard us. I was singing Kambhoji raga alapana, which I had planned to sing for ten minutes, but then my accompanists started to nod vigorously, asking me to stop. I didn't know then that you were not supposed to elaborate a raga for Ilaya Bharatham, you had to sing only the songs. But then when I looked around, TVG was nodding along, signalling that I keep singing the ragam. He wanted to keep listening. I wrapped up in five minutes somehow and moved on to the next song.

Later, at an AIR music competition, I had to sing two songs. We could choose whatever raga and swara we liked. The selected candidates' names were announced in the newspapers, which was a big inducement for competing. For two days, I practised diligently, following Rukmini paati's advice. I selected Mohanam and Bhairavi ragas, choosing Kapali and Upacharamu as my songs, and set the swaras accordingly.

I loved a recording of Santhanam's rendition of the song 'Nannu Palimpa' in Mohanam, and incorporated some of his korvais (rhythmic patterns) as I sang. A month later, the results were announced, and I had won the first prize. M.S. Subbulakshmi attended the prize distribution at the Academy, and I sang for a few minutes, and we all got to take a photo with MS that day.

Just a month later, I applied for a scholarship from the Maharajapuram Viswanatha Iyer Trust. It offered Rs 200 a month for two years. I applied and went in for the selection. After I finished singing, Santhanam asked me, 'Are you the one that got the All India Radio first prize? You sang Kapali, right?' I was surprised, but then realised that he must have been one of the judges to whom my recording for the contest had been sent (they were blind submissions), and I had, quite by chance, chosen one of his trademark songs to perform!

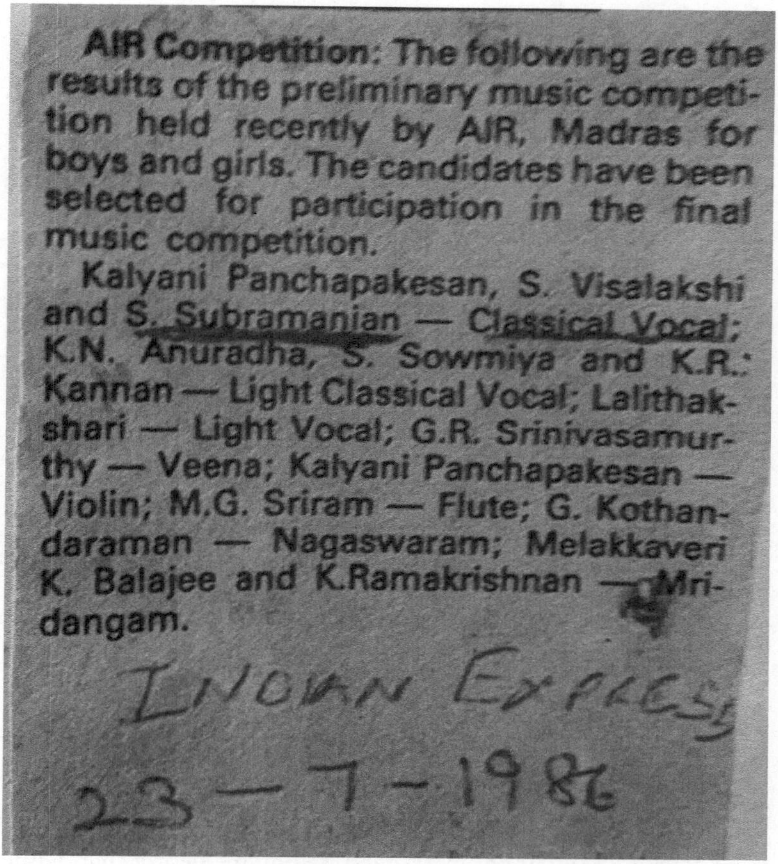

AIR Competition: The following are the results of the preliminary music competition held recently by AIR, Madras for boys and girls. The candidates have been selected for participation in the final music competition.

Kalyani Panchapakesan, S. Visalakshi and S. Subramanian — Classical Vocal; K.N. Anuradha, S. Sowmiya and K.R. Kannan — Light Classical Vocal; Lalithakshari — Light Vocal; G.R. Srinivasamurthy — Veena; Kalyani Panchapakesan — Violin; M.G. Sriram — Flute; G. Kothandaraman — Nagaswaram; Melakkaveri K. Balajee and K.Ramakrishnan — Mridangam.

INDIAN EXPRESS

23 — 7 — 1986

Singing for radio, name in the papers, the early highs of performing

For this scholarship, singers TMT and Rajam Iyer and the violinist T. Rukmini were the judges, with Santhanam often joining them. There were evaluations every six months, with a beautifully designed syllabus defining what we had to sing. At the end of the two-year scholarship, we were all given a concert at Sastry Hall. There were five of us initially, but two were sent off due to a lack of progress, leaving only three of us for the final programme.

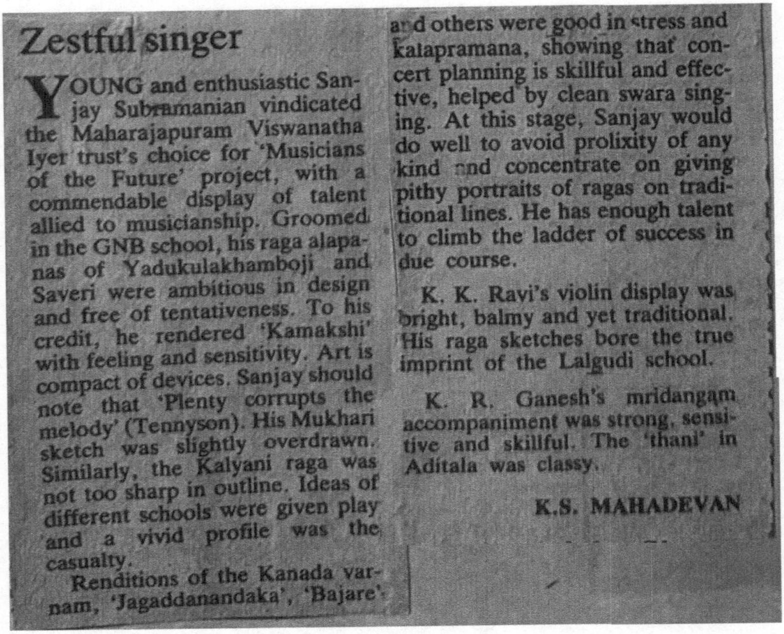

Zestful singer

YOUNG and enthusiastic Sanjay Subramanian vindicated the Maharajapuram Viswanatha Iyer trust's choice for 'Musicians of the Future' project, with a commendable display of talent allied to musicianship. Groomed in the GNB school, his raga alapanas of Yadukulakhamboji and Saveri were ambitious in design and free of tentativeness. To his credit, he rendered 'Kamakshi' with feeling and sensitivity. Art is compact of devices. Sanjay should note that 'Plenty corrupts the melody' (Tennyson). His Mukhari sketch was slightly overdrawn. Similarly, the Kalyani raga was not too sharp in outline. Ideas of different schools were given play and a vivid profile was the casualty.

Renditions of the Kanada varnam, 'Jagaddanandaka', 'Bajare' and others were good in stress and kalapramana, showing that concert planning is skillful and effective, helped by clean swara singing. At this stage, Sanjay would do well to avoid prolixity of any kind and concentrate on giving pithy portraits of ragas on traditional lines. He has enough talent to climb the ladder of success in due course.

K. K. Ravi's violin display was bright, balmy and yet traditional. His raga sketches bore the true imprint of the Lalgudi school.

K. R. Ganesh's mridangam accompaniment was strong, sensitive and skillful. The 'thani' in Aditala was classy.

K.S. MAHADEVAN

A review of my concert for the Maharajapuram Viswanatha Iyer Trust

One day, during this process, I was taking notations while Rajam Iyer was singing. He stopped and pointed out a mistake in my notation. Santhanam intervened, telling me gently that, while my singing was good, learning to notate would help me sing more comfortably. Being a practising artist, Santhanam valued the music, whereas Rajam Iyer, who worked in a college, was more focused on correctness and theory. This balance of practical and theoretical perspectives during the course of the scholarship kept me hooked.

I shared many such moments with Santhanam over the years. Once, in Bangalore, at a competition conducted by the East Cultural Association, a group of us, including Anuradha Sriram and R. Ganesh were participating. The first prize was Rs 1,000, and we had travelled from Madras to compete. Santhanam was one of the judges.

We had to sing a raga picked by the judges. The finalists included Anuradha, Ganesh, myself and two other girls from Bangalore. Anuradha sang first. She was learning from the vocalist Kalyana Raman then. She was asked to sing Saveri. She did a terrific job, singing 'Sankari Sankuru' with many good sangathis. When it was my turn, Santhanam asked me to sing a song in Reetigowla. I didn't know a single keerthanam in the raga back then. I elaborated the raga. Then he asked me to take a line from the song and perform neraval. I had to admit that I didn't know any keerthanams in Reetigowla. Santhanam said, 'What is this pa?' and then sang the line 'sharanagata bharanotsuka' from 'Paripalaya'. 'You've heard this song right, now do the neraval.' I would have been more comfortable if I had been asked to sing ragas I knew well, like Kambhoji or Bhairavi. Somehow though, I managed to complete the song based on his prompt. This is how it was in competitions—anything could happen, and you had to be prepared for the unexpected. Anuradha won the first prize that day; I won second, and went home with Rs 500.

I don't think I would have known so much music as early on as I did if Appa had not turned on the radio whenever he was at home. My dad was a compulsive radio listener. Amma told me that, early on their in their marriage, the Vividh Bharati channel was always on at home. However, after his nearly four-year stint in Calcutta and return to Chennai, I never heard him listen to film music. Vividh Bharati was like a 'blocked' channel on our radio in the mid- to late seventies and early eighties for some reason. Instead, from 1975 to the time I got married in 1993, I listened to an unbelievable amount of Carnatic music on the radio, largely thanks to my father.

The first Carnatic music programme for the day, during our growing-up years, was Isai Amudham, 7–7.15 a.m. They regularly played recordings of the great masters. I still remember enjoying a special offbeat record featuring singer-actress N.C. Vasanthakokilam and Mysore Raja Iyengar's 'Jagadoddharana'. Then came the 8–9 a.m. Arangisai show. Appa would switch the radio off at 7.15 a.m., while he read the paper and we got ready to go to school. Just as we sat down to eat breakfast, he would saunter in and switch on Madras A again for Arangisai. Of course, some days he may have read in advance that it was someone he did not want to listen to, and on those days, the radio would be silent. My school bus came at around 8.30 a.m., and so I heard the first three songs before running off to school. The announcements that preceded the concerts were our main source of information for the names of songs, ragas and composers. V. Thiagarajan, Coimbatore B. Dakshinamoorthy, Madras A. Kannan, Ramanathapuram M.N. Kandaswamy, Palghat Sundaram and V. Nagarajan were all as familiar to me as Dennis Lillee, Andy Roberts or Sunil Gavaskar from a young age.

Then, in the early eighties, when FM radio was first introduced, I had this friend who was crazy about Hindustani music. He would record and share with me programmes featuring artists like V.D. Paluskar, Jitendra Abhisheki, Mallikarjun Mansoor, Basavraj Rajguru and Siyaram Tiwari. He was also a fan of the RTPs that were broadcast once a month. Around that time, my dad had received a cassette player from England, and I finally got a chance to record on my own—an Arangisai concert by Dr Balamuralikrishna, in which he sang 'Kamalambam Bhajare' and 'Ganamalichi' (his own composition in Kalyanavasantham). I still remember the cassette: a TDK D-C90 that Amma had got from a friend in Malaysia. After the one-hour programme, there was still space left on the cassette, so the next day, I recorded the last half hour of a Trichur Ramachandran concert, which featured Bhairavi—Balagopala and a slokam.

Many years later, I was just leaving home for a radio programme when Appa asked me where I was going. I told him I had a live programme. He said, 'This morning? At 8.30? Arangisai? After listening to GNB, MLV and Semmangudi, I have to listen to you now?!'

CHAPTER 5

The Art of Making Music and Friends

My grandfather, Thyagu thaatha, was not only a master storyteller but also a gifted musician. Despite lacking formal training and an understanding of talam or Carnatic songs, his ability to effortlessly sing a fifteen-minute alapana in Todi rivalled that of seasoned professionals. When I was still learning, whenever he heard me practise at home, he'd come join me. 'Sing Todi ra,' he would ask. I've heard from many people, including from a rowdy uncle of mine, Ramudu, that thaatha's Todi was so good that even GNB, who knew him, appreciated it. Thaatha liked it a lot too that people called him 'Todi' Thyagu. My paati, chithis, maamas everyone acknowledged him as the family's master raga singer.

Back when I first started singing concerts, I instinctively reached for his techniques from long years ago. I certainly inherited some nuances of raga singing, be it Todi, Shankarabharanam or Ritigowla, from him. I also picked up enunciations from him, like the sounds mm, aa, ta, na, some syllables and even swara phrases. Even now, when I sing Ritigowla, my style, my phrasing, it is all him. Thaatha also liked to sing slokas, like Vallalar's 'Kodaiyile Ilaipaatri' and the Sanskrit sloka 'Vande Mataram'. Viruthams and slokas weren't usually a part of the younger singers' repertoires, especially among those of us who performed in the afternoons. I began singing them on thaatha's advice. In 1988, for an afternoon kutcheri at Narada Gana Sabha, I sang a virutham which received loud applause, unforgettable even after all these years. The next day, I was thrilled to hear my guru say, 'You are turning out to be a virutham specialist.' Both raga singing and viruthams were gifts from my grandfather to me. He also loved interacting with my musical colleagues. Whenever a violinist or percussionist came home, he'd sing something for them. One of them would eventually remark, 'Even professional vidwans don't sing like this these days.' He would feel smug about it too—'Did you hear that?' he'd ask me.

My father's youngest brother, Ramesh chittappa and his friend from Calcutta, Sivaramakrishnan, too were huge influences on my creative process in the early years. My uncle couldn't sing, but he was a crazy listener, and he knew his music. I think he broke at least ten tape recorders using the rewind button over and over again. In the eighties, before internet and YouTube, he would source precious recordings for me. He constantly challenged me with his deep knowledge and technical insights, gleaned from years of listening. In the early 2000s, he created a brilliant sruti bhedam (where you shift the shadjam of a raga to arrive at a new raga) software on Excel and demonstrated it to almost every prominent Carnatic musician of the time, including legends like Lalgudi Jayaraman and Balamuralikrishna. His friend Sivaramakrishnan maama was a great collector of tapes. No matter what song I wanted, he'd have a tape. I asked him once, 'Maama, do you have GNB's Sarvantaryami?' He said, 'Yes, he has sung it, but I don't have that recording. But I have Vasanthakumari's.' Years later, one day finally he said to me, 'Look, I have your tape also!' Sivaramakrishnan was even older than my father.

It was music that brought these enduring relationships with people much older (or these days way younger) than me into my life. Jegatheeswaran, almost as old as my father, too was very important to me. His passing in 2002 left a deep void in my life as well as music. He was one of my closest musical friends in the most personal way. He even taught me how to tune a tambura. He patiently watched as I learnt and grew in my music over the years. From our first meeting in the early eighties until the end, he was an integral part of my life. Whether gently admonishing me for my idiosyncrasies on stage, suggesting ways to expand my musical repertoire or supporting my ambitious musical forays, he was always there for me.

He loved music and Madras in equal measure. I knew Jega's sister, the violinist Vijayalakshmi Kulaveerasingam, well, and his other sister, Rani, who pursued a career as a Montessori instructor, even stayed with us when I was younger. Whenever he visited Madras, Jega stayed at the Woodlands Hotel and invited me to join him. Our meetings were always musical. He would play the tambura while I sang. He would even record our sessions. The whole thing would last an hour. During those hours, he shared a lot of his knowledge with me. He would ask me to break out of my orthodox thinking about certain ragas and recommend songs for me to sing. He wanted me to work on my voice and would also give me feedback on my concerts, which I really appreciated.

As Jega's health declined in the 1990s, I made it a ritual to bring breakfast from home for him since he could no longer eat at restaurants. Our routine remained unchanged for a few years—he would enjoy my singing, and I would savour Woodlands's signature hot pongal vada afterwards. During December concerts, he was always in attendance, ensuring that my tambura was properly tuned. He generously shared his knowledge with my students, Rethas and Rahul, teaching them the art of stringing the tambura.

For a decade thereafter, Jega, who was originally from Malaysia, made Chennai his home, renting an apartment in Alwarpet. Our bond deepened as I visited him regularly, and he organised chamber concerts for me, and suggested themes and requested songs close to his heart. Jega had a knack for recognising potential in others. He took a neighbour of mine, a neighbour's man Friday named Murugan, under his wing, teaching him to string the tambura and nurturing him into a talented tambura artist.

When I performed in the afternoon slots, I refrained from asking senior artists to accompany me, unless the sabha initiated the conversation; if they did, I would of course gladly accept the proposition. This is how, in 1993, T.K. Murthy maama, Palghat Raghu and Vellore Ramabhadran, all senior mridangam artists played in my concerts. Even though a few senior violinists had accompanied me, Nagai Muralidharan—who would come to have a major influence on my music—hadn't so far. When the vocalist V. Ramachadran's concert was cancelled at the last minute in Bangalore, the organisers of the music festival asked me to fill in. I wanted to turn them down because the invitation was an afterthought, but I agreed when they insisted. Nagai Muralidharan was slated to perform as an accompanist on the violin. I asked the organisers to check if he was okay with it. When the organisers called Nagai Anna (which is what I've always called him), he told them, 'Ask him to call me.' When I did, he said to me most gracefully, 'I am happy to play for you pa, you sing like Kalyana Raman.'

Over the next few years, we slowly developed a pretty close bond. In 2004, Nagai Anna and I embarked on an ambitious thirty-three-kutcheri tour to the US. This tour marked a significant musical breakthrough for me. Until then, I had been relatively conservative in my choice of repertoire, ragas and the musicians I followed, as well as in my thinking and singing.

Despite my guru's teachings, I had not consciously embraced his modern ideas. KSK maama's death in 1999 left me adrift, unsure of my musical path. I was no longer learning from Rukmini paati, my guru had passed away, and I was left feeling unmoored. However, around 2002, encountering SRD introduced a new dimension to my music through the nadaswaram, albeit still within a conservative framework. It was finally the collaboration with Nagai Muralidharan during those years that brought about a huge shift in my music. His approach even to the most traditionally conservative ragas exuded a certain modernity, but it was never over-the-top or contrived. His music practice was almost unconscious, one that evolved from his own experiences, ideas and what his guru followed. It was very rounded, but also very cutting edge.

The concept of modernity I am referring to here, from a purely aesthetic framework, relates to ragas. During raga elaboration, artists employ different techniques to bring out its flavours. From the nuances of gamakas to the strategic interplay of note combinations, musicians have ways to shape the portrayal of a raga, and this ultimately defines the musician's own aesthetic. As a practitioner, one is instinctively attuned to these subtleties. A discerning ear can distinguish between the familiar and the unfamiliar. So, when you listen to something, you know this is from here; this is not from here; this is familiar territory; this is absolutely new; this I can accept today; this I couldn't accept then, but I'm accepting today. When I was young, conservative-thinking in Carnatic music was very strong in me. Even in my listening there were contradictions. For instance, the music I learnt from my grandaunt had a rigid, conservative element, but it was also influenced heavily by GNB's music. By the time I was learning music, GNB's ideas had become more mainstream, but in his own time, he was considered modern. What is considered modern and conservative even within classical music keeps shifting in this manner.

In most kutcheris, singers pay little attention to what the violinist is playing, because they are preoccupied with their own singing. Having observed this, I began to make it a point in concerts to keep my ears always open to both accompanists. Whenever Nagai Anna played for me, my ears were extra sharp. I would sing a sangathi, and he would give it a small twist in his response towards the end—very exhilarating as it unfolded on stage. He'd play a sangathi and look at me. I'd immediately want to use that material, sometimes I would go on to build on that phrase. But most of all, I would hear it and acknowledge it right there on stage. He liked that as well.

We understood and related to each other musically. During that long tour of ours, I learnt a lot of keerthanams from him. He'd sing Koteeswara Iyer songs, and I'd notate them right away. I still sing a lot of pallavis that he set to tune. He, in turn, liked to learn the keerthanams that I set to tune. Just from playing at a great number of concerts together, we developed a strong relationship, musically especially, over many years. Even today, on Vijayadasami I go to see him to offer my namaskaram. I think of him as no less than a guru. Even if we don't perform so much together anymore, we've managed to keep that relationship intact. I still have him listen to anything I have tuned, and if he listens to something I have sung, he'll call and say, 'I heard your song ...'

The early 2000s was musically a very alive time for me. Flute Ramani sir, Nagai Anna and I were like a little gang back in the day. Whenever we met, we would sit together and talk music. Ramani sir would call me often to discuss a kanakku, and say, 'Check if this adds up pa.' I even wrote the sahithyam for one of his pallavis.

Prince Rama Varma has been another significant and unique creative influence on me. We are both of the same age, and it was commonly known that he was a student of Balamurali and hailed from the Travancore royal family, while I remained entangled in the Mylapore music rigamarole. This created a sense of distance between us, despite our shared interests and backgrounds. Once, during a performance at the Swathi Thirunal Sangeetha Sabha in Trivandrum, he was in the audience, occupying a seat in the front row. At the time, I had this rather assertive demeanour.

I thought to myself, 'Oh, this fellow, so what if he's a raja!' Even now he jokes that the first day he met me, I had this big moustache and stared and stared at him during the concert. Later, he invited me to perform at the Navarathri Mandapam, where I sang Swati Thirunal's compositions. While he did tell me he enjoyed the performance, he also had this remarkable knack for giving me constructive criticism that was both gentle and thought-provoking. After my concert that day, he said, 'Your rendition of ragas and swaras is truly beautiful. Though if you paid a tad more attention to the sahithyam, it would elevate your music to even greater heights.' Essentially, he was saying, 'You're really mucking up the words, shouldn't you have read a book and come to sing?' Only said with great finesse. I didn't dismiss his feedback because I am inherently quite self-critical. Even as I prepared for the performance, I had been aware of the issue he highlighted, but at that moment, I'd brushed it aside as insignificant. I realised even then that I needed to adopt a more responsible approach as a singer. What he said turned out to be an eye-opener.

I was already grappling with the influence of Nagai Anna at the time. As I introspected more deeply about my music, I found myself incorporating various nuevo elements into my performances. (Anything new that hasn't been done before becomes nuevo or modern in a classical context. This could be the choice of ragas for elaboration, the use of musical phrases that challenge the orthodoxy or just vocal mannerisms or graces that sound unlike what has been done before. Many great musicians of the past have incorporated nuevo elements, things that were seen as unconventional in their time, into their work. Be it composers like Thyagaraja or Muthiah Bhagavatar or Balamuralikrishna, or singers like GNB or instrumental artists like Rajaratnam Pillai or Manpoondia Pillai, their innovations were once novel. Over time what was nuevo becomes accepted in tradition.) When I began adding a few Balamurali compositions into my repertoire, Rama Varma expressed his appreciation, and that furthered our musical connection. He shared recordings and tapes with me that he thought I might enjoy. Then our friendship blossomed beyond music; we shared a mutual love of food and often exchanged humorous messages via SMS back in the day. Over more than two decades, we've built up a healthy camaraderie.

It was during those years that I transitioned from being a strict conservative to embracing a slightly more liberated, out-of-the-box approach. I experimented with new ideas and took liberties with my performances without getting bogged down by the dilemma of whether innovation was right or wrong. Throughout this journey, all of these artists stood by me unwaveringly. Not one of them questioned my artistic choices because they valued my artistry just as much they did our friendship. Ultimately, it seemed to resonate with audiences as well. My repertoire evolved; I began tuning pallavis in Hindustani ragas and exploring more vivadis. There are a set of ragas called 'vivadi' because they contain dissonant notes (where the Ga note becomes Ri note or the Ri note becomes Ga note, etc.). These ragas were shunned by Carnatic musicians in concerts. Some top musicians felt singing vivadi was inauspicious (or caused dosha) and was not good for the musician's health, or that it could lead to untimely death. However, KSK maama believed that those who didn't know to sing these ragas came up with these excuses. To me, it didn't matter if it was vivadi or not. It was all the same. If I liked a raga at a given point in time, I wanted to sing it. Rama Varma's validation as I was moving towards this kind of new artistic space meant a lot to me, not only because it was coming from someone close to me but also because he was someone who possessed profound musical insight.

Rama Varma is a very involved singer; he knows exactly what he's singing but he likes to make it as accessible as possible. His style is different from traditional concerts. He laces his concerts with stories, talking about the songs, the composer, talking about his experiences with the music, etc. He makes it a very engaging and entertaining experience. Anybody can come and have a good time. At the same time, he does not compromise at all on the quality of his singing. He sings the lyrics perfectly—it is in rhythm—and he doesn't take any musical phrase for granted. When I received the Kalanidhi Award, I specifically requested Rama Varma to speak about me. Some people asked me why I didn't choose a more senior figure, but I preferred to have my contemporary and equal share his perspective. His speech was both eloquent and humorous, and he jokingly remarked that it was perhaps this speech, rather than his performances, that earned him more recognition at the Academy.

Around the time I received the Sangita Kalanidhi, my reputation for singing Tamil songs had solidified in my home state. Ever since, I've had this strong desire to expand my repertoire to other South Indian languages. While my progress with Kannada songs has been gradual compared to Tamil, I am now starting to see tangible results. I've immersed myself in the poetry of Akkamahadevi and Basavanna's vachanas. I also tuned a Rashtrakavi Kuvempu song, 'O Nanna Chethana', recently.

It's essential to keep setting new creative goals to inject freshness into one's craft. I want to cultivate a unique repertoire that resonates with audiences across the South. As I explore these languages, I am also adamant about not merely singing the traditional songs but creating my own. This involves retuning songs and reimagining compositions to align with my ideas. I also have to have a comfort with the lyrical aesthetic, so I am looking at songs from the last two hundred years. Since Carnatic music has an abundance of bhakti in its repertoire already, when I search for newer lyrics to sing, I like to explore words that seem to critique society. The social criticism of Vallalar, Akkamahadevi and Basavanna are relevant to this day, which is why they appeal to my sensibilities.

What's also interesting and exciting for me now are my ventures outside of traditional kutcheris. Collaborating with music composer Sean Roldan has opened up a world of opportunities. From working on film songs and projects like Coke Studio, I'm gradually expanding my horizon. One of my favourite recent projects with Roldan is an album of Vallalar songs, *Anbenum Peruveli* (The Grand Expanse Called Love). In it, I explore completely new genres, ranging from rock to pop and jazz, all in Tamil. While Carnatic influences are strewn across the songs, the album is a departure from the familiar and marks a new phase in my career. Personally, it's been a life-changing experience for me, stepping out of that conservative space that I've occupied all my life.

Thinking back, after receiving the Sangita Kalanidhi, I came to realise that I was entering a stage where I might eventually sing a film song. I had evolved from the person who said, 'I absolutely will not do it.' I understood that, at this stage in my life, I didn't have to hold on to such rigid beliefs.

During the pandemic, when I wasn't performing at all, I received a call to sing for an advertisement. That never materialised.

Then I decided to reach out to Sean Roldan, who had learnt music from me and whose music I admired. Instead of approaching the likes of Ilaiyaraja or Rahman right at the outset, I thought it might be easier to collaborate with someone I knew. It was again Aravind S.A., the stand-up comedian, who encouraged me to stop thinking about it and take action. He said that Sean was my disciple, and asked why I was hesitant, and finally insisted that I call him, almost (but not literally) at gunpoint. In hindsight, I am glad he did that.

Sean was thrilled to receive my call, and over the next three months, we had three to four sessions together. Initially, he had me sing classical songs to understand my mindset. I made it clear to him that I was open to singing any genre of music, not just Carnatic. I considered myself a singer first and foremost, not just a Carnatic musician. I told him that while I would continue to sing Carnatic music and perform concerts, I was willing to explore other styles as well.

I asked Sean to assess whether my singing was suitable for the kind of collaboration we were considering. If it wasn't, I was prepared to return to what I was doing before. He reassured me that there was no need for doubt and that he believed our collaboration would yield great results.

Having been immersed in the Carnatic space for so long, my writing style too was quite traditional. When composing a pallavi, for example, I would typically use formal Tamil or classical-sounding language. But now, collaborating with artists from different genres has helped me transition to writing in modern Tamil more seamlessly.

In one of the promos for my shows, I sang 'Nadapaduve Nadakkum Que Sera Sera', and it flowed effortlessly. I translated Shakespeare's 'All the world's a stage, and all the men and women its players' to 'Ulagame, oru medai' and sang a pallavi. These transitions have become easier because of my interactions and collaborations with artists outside the Carnatic sphere. I've even incorporated lines from songs by the band Sean Roldan & Friends into my performances.

These days, if I come across something I like, I freely use it in my classical concerts. This exchange between different musical worlds has been incredibly enriching for me.

CHAPTER 6

The Kalanidhi and After

I began performing at the Academy during the season in 1989. The YACM championed my cause with the Academy for the much sought-after afternoon slot for young artists. Back in those years, famous gurus who wanted their proteges to have these slots would call in favours with the sabhas, so slots were hard to come by. Luckily for me, the Music Academy had begun to recognise the YACM's role as a conduit for emerging talents around this time, and so their lobbying helped me get that space, marking a departure from the norm.

It is another matter that I used to haunt the Academy, when I was still playing the violin, well before I became a performer. The December of 1977 was memorable. There was such a buzz at home, for MS was going to perform at the Academy after a hiatus. My paternal grandparents visited us from Calcutta to attend the season every year back then. My grandfather had been away for a couple of days the previous year, and I had claimed his ticket and heard M.D. Ramanathan and TMT. Those were some of my earliest experiences of the primetime evening concert at the Academy. This year, I was keen on attending MS's concert, but tickets were

YOUTH ASSOCIATION FOR CLASSICAL MUSIC
25th October 1986
7.30.P.M..-.9-P.M.

S.Subrahmanyam	-	Vocal
M.A.Krishnaswamy	-	Violin
S.Sivakumar	-	Mridangam

1. Varnam - Todi - Adi - Patnam Subramanya Iyer

2. Gajavadana - Sriranjani- Adi - Papanasam Sivan

   Meaning:Lord Ganesa, abode of mercy, son of Shiva, beautiful one. You, who have been worshipped by all including the Devas and rishies, I surrender myself to your lotus feet. You are the base for the three worlds, the essence of Shivagana mantras, the thread of my lifeline; Bless me O Omkara

3. Evarikai - Devamanohari - M.Chapu - Thyagaraja

   Meaning: O Lord Rama, for whom did you take this avatharam ? I salute the great saint who called you to this world. With the name described in the vedas; with a body superior to that of Brahma and Shiva; with your history being the abode of happiness; and in the role of a Rajarishi, for whom did you take this avatharam ?

4. Kapali - Mohanam - Adi - Papanasam Sivan

   Meaning: O Kapaleeswara, your face exhibits compassion; Saviour of all, saluted by the people of earth, the kings and the eight Digbalas. Having the crescent on your head, snakes adorning your neck; wearing a garland of skulls and the skin of an elephant, having the drum which produces an earth shattering sound and the Trishul, your skin, smeared with ashes, glitters and captures the heart of women.

5. Vararaga - Senchu Kambojhi - Adi - Thyagaraja

   Meaning: Without knowing anything about swaram,raagam or moorchanai, there are several Raga, Tala vidwans whoo have the foolish notion of thinking that they are the greatest. These persons who are not interestted in knowing that the sounds produced by the body are nothing but the forms of the pranava. These people can only harm others.

6. Upacharamu - Bhairavi - Adi - Thyagaraja

   Meaning: O Rama, your dress exhibits the bright light of lightning you, who have slept on the Adisesha, take pity onme and accept my offerings and services. You, who have dominated this world and given whatever asked for; The golden umbrella studded with the Navaratnas is reserved only for you.

7. Kamalappadha - Harikambhoji - Adi - Papanasam Sivan

   Meaning: Lord Muruga whohas the lotus feet which I cannot forget. You who have been praised by the devas as the compassionate one, one,who is capable of releasing me from this cycle of life and death. In this wonderful human is wasted by spending the days idly, how can the eternal joy be enjoyed. O nephew of Lord Vishnu, born in the Sharavana tank, Protector of Devas, son of Lord Shiva, shower thy blessings.

8. Slokam - Ragamalika

9. Mangalam

Demystifying the song list for my YACM concert

sold out, and it was impossible to get hold of one. Meanwhile, my mother, in a moment of whimsy, decided to complicate things by imposing a condition: I could go to the concert if I sat and played the Shankarabharanam varnam a hundred times on my violin. I still cannot believe that I did this. That December, I played 'Saami Ninne' a hundred times, but alas, there were just no tickets, and I could not make it to the concert. Thankfully for me, my great-great-grandfather worked for the renowned Hoe & Co., the famous diary makers. Emberumanar Chettiar, the President of the Indian Fine Arts Society and the owner of Hoe & Co., used to send my grandfather a couple of complimentary tickets for their annual festival at Vani Mahal. That year, MS was performing there as well, so I was in luck. The only song I distinctly remember from that concert was 'Manavyala' in Nalinakanti raga because I had just learnt it at the time. Of course, another memorable moment was when she brought out the jalra, hand-held cymbals that helped keep time, while singing the lighter pieces.

One particular late-night kutcheri of Sankaranarayanan stands out vividly too. I count it among the most memorable concerts I've ever heard; I particularly remember his splendid 'Eppo Varuvaro'. I've watched Vyjayanthimala dance, sat on the stage and heard Madurai Somu sing, and there was this one MLV concert in which she was accompanied by Kanyakumari on violin, T.R. Rajamani, Mani Iyer's son, on the mridangam and Harishankar on the kanjira. It was even telecast live on Doordarshan. For this one too I had a stage ticket. (For very popular artists, when the hall is sold out, sabhas offer low-priced tickets so you can sit on the stage, on the floor, on either side of the performers.) I watched the entire concert from up on the stage, and when my face was shown on the telecast, all my neighbours were excited. After all these years, I can still recall what songs were sung, and what it felt like to be in the hall that day.

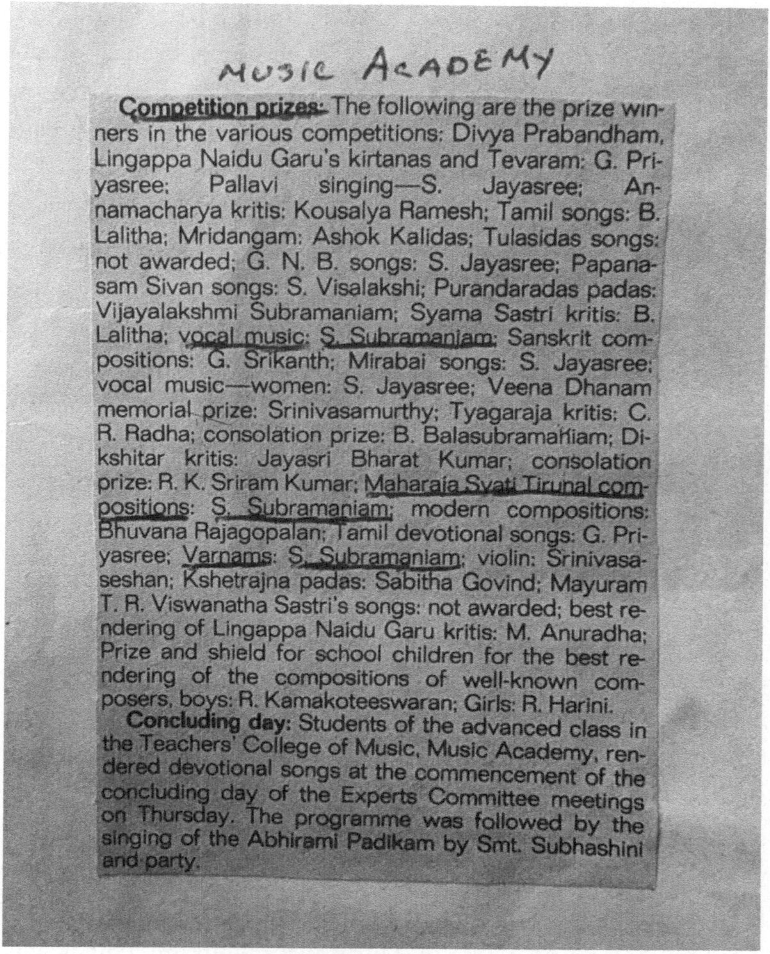

MUSIC ACADEMY

Competition prizes: The following are the prize winners in the various competitions: Divya Prabandham, Lingappa Naidu Garu's kirtanas and Tevaram: G. Priyasree; Pallavi singing—S. Jayasree; Annamacharya kritis: Kousalya Ramesh; Tamil songs: B. Lalitha; Mridangam: Ashok Kalidas; Tulasidas songs: not awarded; G. N. B. songs: S. Jayasree; Papanasam Sivan songs: S. Visalakshi; Purandaradas padas: Vijayalakshmi Subramaniam; Syama Sastri kritis: B. Lalitha; vocal music: S. Subramaniam; Sanskrit compositions: G. Srikanth; Mirabai songs: S. Jayasree; vocal music—women: S. Jayasree; Veena Dhanam memorial prize: Srinivasamurthy; Tyagaraja kritis: C. R. Radha; consolation prize: B. Balasubramaniam; Dikshitar kritis: Jayasri Bharat Kumar; consolation prize: R. K. Sriram Kumar; Maharaja Svati Tirunal compositions: S. Subramaniam; modern compositions: Bhuvana Rajagopalan; Tamil devotional songs: G. Priyasree; Varnams: S. Subramaniam; violin: Srinivasaseshan; Kshetrajna padas: Sabitha Govind; Mayuram T. R. Viswanatha Sastri's songs: not awarded; best rendering of Lingappa Naidu Garu kritis: M. Anuradha; Prize and shield for school children for the best rendering of the compositions of well-known composers, boys: R. Kamakoteeswaran; Girls: R. Harini.

Concluding day: Students of the advanced class in the Teachers' College of Music, Music Academy, rendered devotional songs at the commencement of the concluding day of the Experts Committee meetings on Thursday. The programme was followed by the singing of the Abhirami Padikam by Smt. Subhashini and party.

An early win at an 'Academy' contest

As I grew into my singing years and realised that I was going to be a practitioner, it naturally became my goal to sing in the December season, and the Academy has always been the centrepiece of the season. Before the Academy, I had lent my voice to four sabhas, Kartik Fine Arts, Kalarasana, Krishna Gana Sabha (though not in the season but during Gokulashtami) and Mylapore Fine Arts. My performance at the Academy finally had a ripple effect on the other establishments. Other sabhas felt compelled to invite me to perform when I was given an afternoon slot at the Academy, with Narada Gana Sabha being among the last to extend the offer.

Back then, the musicians who handled the afternoon slots for concert organisers would fill the schedule up with those they favoured. If you didn't know them, or if you were not on talking terms with the organisers, they were likely to ignore you. At Kalarasana, for instance, I sang one year, and then didn't for a couple of years after. One time, I was at Karaikudi Mani's residence when the Kalarasana's secretary telephoned him. It showed me clearly how arbitrary these selections tend to be. Karaikudi Mani named one musician after another, asked for Hyderabad Brothers to be included in the festival as well, and then he inquired if I was interested. I politely declined. As I've mentioned before, I wanted the sabha to call me.

But once I sang at the Academy, there was no need for these personal connections or favouritism to play out. Organisers from outside Chennai too attended the Academy's concerts to book performers for their events. In 1990, for instance, as soon as I finished a concert, C.S. Krishna Iyer, who was conducting a Thyagaraja Utsavam in Palakkad, booked me right there as I wrapped up. At another afternoon concert, a member of the royal family was around, and they invited me to perform for the Swathi Thirunal Sangeetha Sabha in Thiruvananthapuram. This is why the Academy is so important to a young artist. Performing there in an evening slot eventually, in 1997, marked the beginning of my own understanding that I was there to stay. This music was it. I was not going to give it up. I was a CA then, but more interested in and focused on my music.

Through all these years, even as I performed in the primetime slot, the Kalanidhi honour was not on my radar at all. The question of when one might get such an award is unanswerable. One could make assumptions based on how many people were in line to get it first—too many people, too may equations at play. But all those assumptions changed when the president of the Music Academy, N. Murali, decided to award the Sangita Kalanidhi to Sudha Raghunathan in 2013.

*

The Kalanidhi Award came up only in 1942. Before that, who knows what goals artists may have had. Fame, money? Today, this award is akin to the Oscars for us Carnatic practitioners. It's only an institutional recognition, but it comes from one of the biggest, most respected institutions of its time. The Music Academy was the first institution to organise an Annual Conference for Carnatic music. Prior to the establishment of the Kalanidhi Award, borrowing from colonial traditions, there was the honour of presiding over the conference as its president. Since 1942, the person presiding over the conference has been offered the title 'Kalanidhi' as well.

As for me, I certainly wanted to reach the evening slot where I would be regarded as a professional, and

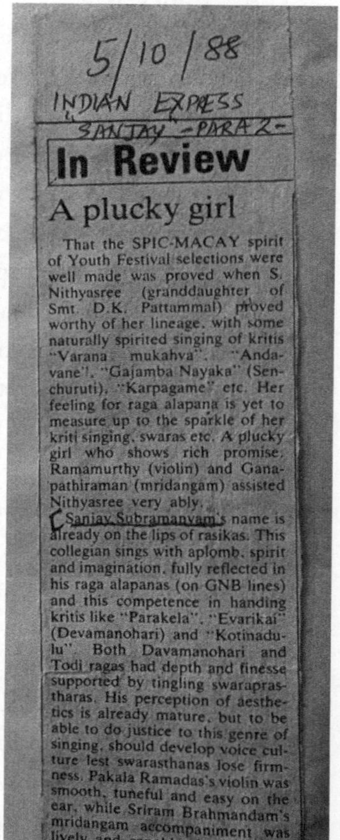

5/10/88
INDIAN EXPRESS
SANJAY - PARA 2 -

In Review

A plucky girl

That the SPIC-MACAY spirit of Youth Festival selections were well made was proved when S. Nithyasree (granddaughter of Smt. D.K. Pattammal) proved worthy of her lineage, with some naturally spirited singing of kritis "Varana mukahva", "Andavane", "Gajamba Nayaka" (Senchuruti), "Karpagame" etc. Her feeling for raga alapana is yet to measure up to the sparkle of her kriti singing, swaras etc. A plucky girl who shows rich promise. Ramamurthy (violin) and Ganapathiraman (mridangam) assisted Nithyasree very ably.

Sanjay Subramanyam's name is already on the lips of rasikas. This collegian sings with aplomb, spirit and imagination, fully reflected in his raga alapanas (on GNB lines) and this competence in handing kritis like "Parakela", "Evarikai" (Devamanohari) and "Kotinadulu". Both Davamanohari and Todi ragas had depth and finesse supported by tingling swaraprastharas. His perception of aesthetics is already mature, but to be able to do justice to this genre of singing, should develop voice culture lest swarasthanas lose firmness. Pakala Ramadas's violin was smooth, tuneful and easy on the ear, while Sriram Brahmandam's mridangam accompaniment was lively and capable throughout.

K.S. MAHADEVAN

A review from the early days

people would pay to listen to me. I wanted to see if I could get the price I demanded. These were one's tangible goals as a musician. Musically though one had and has countless goals. (You wanted to learn a certain number of songs or sing certain types of pallavis at concerts, for instance.) In 2000, I finally quit my day job, which had begun to increasingly feel like a drag. I had reached the evening slot, people were actually paying to hear me sing and I was now making more as a singer than as a chartered accountant.

Three things had happened to birth this transition. First, every day I hated how my day had been spent. 'What am I doing?' became an existential question. I did not enjoy going to the office, meeting people, going out for snacks, having tea, looking at some files ... none of it was interesting. I spent eight years like that. But I had to do it because I had a young family, young kids; we'd bought a house on loan, so there was the EMI to think of. Finally, when my music started picking up, I had to go on tours to the US for concerts for three-and-a-half months at a stretch. My middle-class conscience kicked in then. 'How can I take the firm's money when I'm not working?' But my partners at Karra and Co. were more accommodative of me than I was to myself. They said, 'Who asked you? You can come whenever possible.' In fact, the late R. Sivakumar, one of the partners, even helped me make the right career choice early on, so I could keep performing. If he hadn't stopped me from going to a bank for industrial training, I might have never made it as a singer. The company would have certainly helped me as I climbed up the musical ladder, but I couldn't do it—and that was the second reason. Finally, I also felt that if I quit I could do more justice to my music. All of this was at the back of my mind, I don't think it was a driving force. Yet, the moment I quit, it was as if a switch had been turned on. The improvement in the level of my professional involvement and development in music was instantaneous. I was also doing well professionally as a musician, and I needed that time off. I couldn't just sit at work and not think about music.

Kasturi and Sons Ltd was building a golf course in Odiyur back then. My then boss, Premkumar Karra, said to me one day, 'The Chairman of the Central Bank of India is coming. Why don't you drive down to the spot? You are a musician, and he knows music. I can also introduce you to him; it will be a good PR exercise for our firm.' I drove 95 kms that morning. That evening, I had a concert at Sastry Hall at 6.30 p.m. We waited for the chairman to arrive at 11 a.m. He finally showed up at 3 p.m. I drove like a maniac and reached home by 6.15 p.m., changed and reached Sastry Hall by 6.30 p.m. and performed a full kutcheri. I had all of fifteen minutes to get to the show. I managed to impress my guru that day; he spoke about it a few days later at a lec-dem, 'He drove for so long, went out on work and still sang a good raga.' Still, I decided that this was crazy. I couldn't do it. How could I do justice to my art like this?

Once I quit, I had to think about what I would do with my time. Those days, I was teaching a lot too. So, students would come home. I thought of it as a brand-building exercise, if these students went out and performed well on stage, that would reflect well on me too. My own kids were young, so I got to spend a bit of time with them briefly.

I wanted more and more people to come and listen to me sing, and I wanted to hold strong to my identity as a Carnatic musician. Having decided not to sing any other genre, I thought hard about what else I could do and how best I could reach people. My primary driving force in those years was the simple fact that I liked to sing, and I liked that people listened to me sing. Every morning, I looked forward to singing. When I woke up, my first thought would be, 'What should I sing today?' Even today, once I'm up, I look forward to singing more than anything else.

But, to return to the Kalanidhi, until Sudha received the honour, it was reserved for those in their seventies because of this big, long list of artists who had to be given the award. Sudha was still in her fifties. When Murali became the president of the Music Academy, perhaps he wanted to be a little forward-thinking, and he also had a new committee advising him. To the best of my understanding, this is how the award works: the Academy has a president and an executive committee. The president has a very strong voice, but he or she listens to feedback from the committee, and then finally, the committee sits together to take a final call on whom to give the award to each year.

When they conferred the award on her, in fact, Murali called me and asked, 'Sir, we have a plan to give it to Sudha Raghunathan. What do you think? What is your opinion?' That was a big turning point. When he told me they were considering giving it to her, he also added, 'If we give it to her now, you will all get it sooner, or else you will all get it late too!' Until that moment, I thought these honours were for consideration ten to fifteen years down the line. The year after Sudha, TVG received his Kalanidhi. And then I did in 2015.

Guruvayur Dorai, SRD, KSK maama (who was given the Acharya Award instead) and Nagai Anna are among the many artists who are all deserving of the Kalanidhi, in my opinion. As members of the musician community, we don't really have a voice in who is given the award. It is the committee that takes those decisions, but they always try to find out what people think of their choice. Though I have never been a part of the process, when people who are on the committee call me, I do drop in my suggestions for other awards given by the Academy, such as the Acharya and TTK Award.

When artists themselves make a bid for the Kalanidhi, someone will call on their behalf, sometimes even politicians! Everybody

श्री
Music Academy
MADRAS
॥ नादतनुम अनिशं नमामि ॥
birudupatra

We, the President and Members of
The Music Academy Madras and the Members
of the Expert Advisory Committee thereof now assembled in Sadas
at Chennai on 1st January 2016 do hereby confer on you,

Sanjay Subrahmanyan

the birudu of

Sangita Kalanidhi

as a mark of personal distinction and in token thereof we
hereby present to you this Birudupatra and authorise you to
wear the insignia presented to you herewith.

May it please Almighty God to give you long life and strength
to carry on your work for the advancement and propagation
of this Art of all Arts, Indian Music.

89th ANNUAL CONFERENCE & CONCERTS

President
The Music Academy Madras

The 'goal', so to speak

wants a say on who gets the award. How the committee actually decides on the final awardee when there's this much pressure is hard to say, but the general feeling is that if the president is convinced, he or she will work towards a consensus among the members. Very rarely does one find disagreements in the committee, I hear.

Although rumour has it that there was something of a contest in my selection, that some members had proposed an alternate candidate at the last minute. And in the end, they all agreed on my name.

For as long I can remember, I have been curious about who's going to be that year's Kalanidhi, which is true of anyone following the Carnatic music scene. Even people who don't like the Music Academy grudgingly acknowledge the fact of its premier status and the value of its seal of approval.

Receiving the honour was a big, huge high, quite unlike anything I'd felt before. I still think back to that December, when each morning of the season brought a beautiful ritual. Before those 8 a.m. lec-dems, I was greeted by the entire committee, along with the president at 7.25 a.m., and we ate breakfast together. It was a gesture of camaraderie that I cherished deeply. As the Kalanidhi, you have to chair two lec-dems every day and three to four panel discussions through the festival, and offer comments/summaries of each of these.

Even now, as I enter the Academy, the president comes to receive me, a tradition that speaks of their genuine regard. I sang in the evening slot on 27 December the year of my award, and the next morning, I was there at 7.25 a.m. sharp for our breakfast. That day, Murali happened to be late by five minutes and laughed, saying, 'Not bad, sir, the next morning also you're here early!' Long before he became the president, from as long back as 1997, I've seen Murali in the front row for my evening concerts. Even during my afternoon kutcheri days, the then president T.T. Vasu attended every time those of us from the YACM performed. I've always considered myself an 'Academy boy', and I said so while receiving the honour too.

A year before the Kalanidhi, in 2014, the National Eminence Award instituted by Shanmukhananda Sabha, Mumbai, came as a

With Semmangudi Srinivasa Iyer at Shanmukhananda Sabha

surprise. I was thrilled to be joining a lineage that included the likes of Semmangudi, Balamuralikrishna and Pandit Bhimsen Joshi. After the Kalanidhi, I received the Tamil Isai Sangam's honour, the Tamil Isai Perarignar. Needless to say, this was very special to me. In fact, I'd always thought I might receive it before the Kalanidhi. Indian Fine Arts then offered me their Kalasikhamani title. I've had a long relationship with the organisation. Because of our familial connection with Hoe & Co., sentimentally, personally, the award meant a great deal to me.

Once the excitement settled down following these three years, the flurry of calls with awards and honours too subsided. I still receive the occasional offer from smaller sabhas, a title in lieu of a concert, and unless I have a longstanding relationship with the organisation, I end up politely declining such requests.

Immediately after the Kalanidhi Award, I felt the pressure to live up to it. I guess that's only natural. But someone told my mother-in-law something profound back then: 'Listen to him sing from now on; he will be free.' Later, TVG said something similar to me: 'Ey, you can sing happily from now on.' At that time, I didn't fully grasp the significance of what he said, but as I resumed singing, it dawned on me that there had been this subtle pressure lurking in the corners of my mind, a weight that I hadn't fully acknowledged until after I received the honour. It felt like this pressure had been building up inside my head, and come January, it finally burst. Once it was all over, I really was finally singing with a lot of freedom.

The other thing that changed after 2015 was the strong sense of responsibility I felt towards my voice specifically. Until then, my focus was always the content. Raga, keerthanam, swara—the actual musical content and the aesthetics surrounding it. I thought that if I delivered these with my voice, whatever its state, that was enough.

Of course, I knew my voice had rough edges. Until I was at the concert, I couldn't say for sure if I would be able to reach the upper gandharam or madhyamam that day. I would shout or manage somehow to sing the song. TVG even said to me once, 'Somehow you're singing and it's working out so far; be careful.' He knew I was doing a lot of things wrong.

After the Kalanidhi, I started to think about my voice a lot. I have never had a good opinion of it, to be honest—always thought of it as my weakest attribute. Most people I know, including Aarthi, do not agree with that assessment. My close friends and fans insist that it's not true, but my own opinion of my voice has always been very low.

I've felt that it's not up to the mark, that it has issues, but I managed because of my superior ability to interpret the music. I had confidence in that skill. Since I could sing a Sahana, even if my voice was lacking, I knew I would be able to hold the audience. Yet, because of this diffidence regarding my voice, I never felt fully satisfied after a concert. I would think to myself, 'Fine, that was okay.' It was never 'My voice was perfect today.'

Even today, I cannot bring myself to say that. I still have a problem. If someone asked me what I hate the most about myself, I would say 'my voice' without hesitation.

I have problems with how I want to use it, with hitting certain notes, singing certain phrases, how I sing those phrases ... these things continue to trouble me, but I work with it. That's the churning in art. As an artist, you work through these challenges.

For long years, for instance, I was unsatisfied with the way I sang lyrics. The initial decade and a half of my career, I had cared very little for words. There were mistakes in the lyrics I sang in concerts. Not in Tamil, sure, but other languages certainly. My Telugu would sound like Tamil, and it would be all so wrong. After Rama Varma alerted me to this flaw, I have strived to improve my grasp of words.

In my search for a solution to my vocal concerns, I've explored various avenues. I've been reading about it, listening, understanding, even meeting with potential voice trainers. The process is akin to retraining my voice, challenging muscle memory accustomed to years of singing a particular way. Two years ago, just as concerts resumed after the lockdown, I felt as if I had overcome most of my challenges and was on the right path. However, over the course of 2023 and '24, I've noticed a return of some bad singing habits.

Two years ago, when I thought I had made significant improvement in my range, people did notice it. Earlier people would say, 'That Sahana was great', 'Shankarabharanam was lovely' or 'Your singing really touched me; I am so happy to listen to your Tamil songs.' Suddenly, people who were not necessarily into the content of my music were speaking to me about my voice.

But with the return of the cracks in my voice, I would rank December 2023 as my worst season performance in years. I wish there was a way to entirely forget about how my voice fared in it. The feeling that something was wrong plagued me throughout the month, and I spent all of January 2024 trying to figure out what was going wrong.

To address this, I began by looking at literature online, especially Western methods of voice usage. It helped me realise that there is a scientific approach to the matter. I hadn't even thought about these things before. Receiving the Kalanidhi freed me up to these ideas.

Interestingly, this shift was sparked by an interviewer who asked if I looked for music resources online. I said to him, 'Yeah, I listen to all forms of music.' He said, 'No, a musician I interviewed once told me he'd googled "how to sing".' Now why should a singer google how to sing? That question led me down this path of rediscovering my voice. If you had a problem with how you were singing, you would go ask someone. Until then it hadn't even occurred to me that I could google it.

Right after my Kalanidhi concert, this lady came up to me and asked if there was a problem with my voice. It was such a big occasion for me, and at some point in the concert my voice may have faltered, but it was odd that she chose to ask me this question on such a day. But then in some corner of my mind I'd always known that I needed to address the matter at some point. As a singer, you have to see the voice like an instrument.

I began to actively scout around for somebody to help me with voice training. Having decided that I would like to work with somebody locally, I had shortlisted a few names. I was sure I'd find somebody. The young here were smart.

Girish, who composed music for 'Elay Makka', which I sang in Coke Studio Season 2, finally recommended his colleague, Anjana Rajagopalan. She was familiar with Carnatic music and had released a Tamil song in the opera genre, which I found rather beautiful. I've now been working on my voice with her inputs.

Even as I feel more confident now, there are still areas that I would like to work on, especially with regard to hitting the high notes. I know how I was getting there in the past, and that's not the way I want to do it anymore. That method has not been good for my voice in the long run. When I was young, I just brushed this off and went past it, but now I think I shouldn't have. I know that it's a technical adjustment, and I just have to figure out the technique. It is like deadlifting, where you have to learn to activate your core and use your back. It's just some work for my muscles. Anjana is helping me understand how I can use my voice in a scientific manner so that I can get rid of habits that can be injurious to its health. She gives me voice exercises to practise every day, which are easing a great deal of the discomfort and strain I experience while singing. These are usually repetitive warm-up phrases that help my voice, but they tend to sound to others like a cowboy yeehawing in an opera. Venkatesh heard me practise one day and asked, shocked, 'What are you doing?!' Poor guy must have thought I was going to sing that on stage.

CHAPTER 7

The Studio Life

My very first studio experience was at the age of twenty-five, when I recorded for the renowned Sangeetha Cassettes; they'd offered to release an hour-long album. I had to wait until I had reasonable visibility as a performing artist for an audio company to approach me to record a cassette. I'd been promoted to the 1.30 p.m. concert slot in 1992, and my audience during the season had begun to grow. I had already been singing in this slot for two years when I got to record. The payment, a meagre Rs 2,000. Royalties? None.

Until then, Sangeetha Cassettes had used an eight-track system—they recorded each track separately and mixed them all together finally—but my first album coincided with their acquisition of a new Digital Audio Tape (DAT) machine. I was told at the recording, 'This is a two-track machine, we can't mix tracks, because eight tracks are still analogue. We do not have digital eight track mixers yet.' This basically meant that there was no room for editing, mixing or tuning. It would be as if I were singing a concert! The album demanded great precision, and it took me a whole day to record the sixty-minute album. A small hiccup meant the entire piece had to be redone from the top. Music director L. Krishnan, who supervised the album, listened to each song to check if it passed

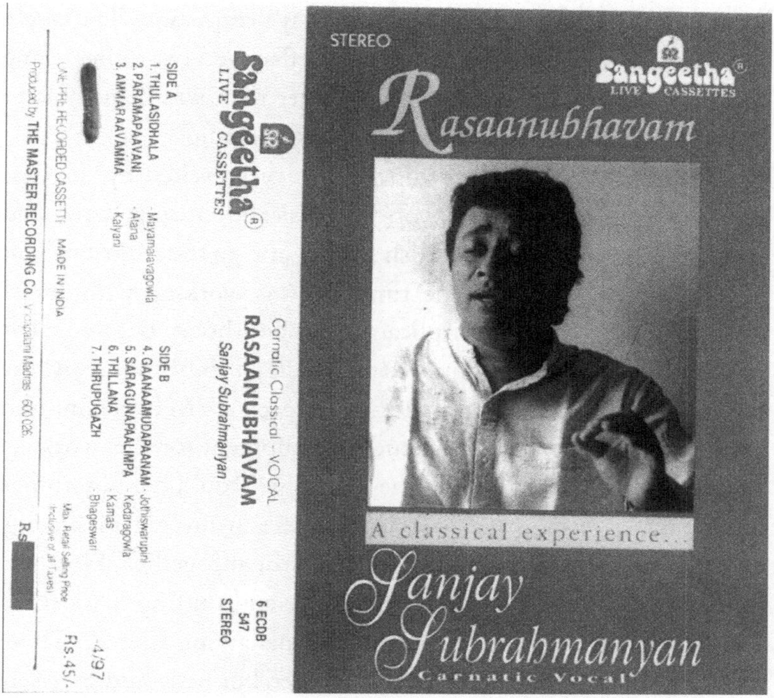

My first album. Photographed for the cover by the legendary Raghavendra Rao

muster. If he was not satisfied, I had to sing again. I still remember, he okayed my 'Amma Ravamma' in the first take, but 'Ganamudha Paanam' took a whopping six takes! The song took seven minutes to complete each time. Every time a scratch or a cough, or a minor shruthi slip-up would come up, we had to perform the entire song again. I sang two such albums for the label without edits and mixes.

I finished recording the first album and shot a professional photograph for the cover. A couple of weeks later, when the album released, Aarthi and I were in Mangalore for a wedding. I went to a music shop—and there it was! What great thrill to see the album in that shop with my photograph. Seeing my music in this tangible form so far away from home quite took my breath away. The label's distribution network was remarkably effective. The other thing that gave me a real kick as a young singer then was being able to listen to myself on those big speakers at the studio.

When I first began recording, I was very excited by the old-fashioned editing, which involved physically cutting tapes and pasting them back. I would finish singing and go to see the brilliant editor Raju at work. At the time, he was working with AVM Studios and lived in the Triplicane neighbourhood. Before he left for work in the morning, musicians would go to his house, where he would do manual editing. He had to reach AVM by 9 a.m., and of course he couldn't use the studio's equipment for this work, so I would go see him at 6.30 in the morning. I could tell him things like 'take the ga ma pa da ni sa from here in my ragam singing, and that ri ga ma ga ri sa, and combine them together'. He knew exactly what to do, cutting it out neatly and putting it together. His father was Sangita Kalanidhi S. Ramanathan, after all. These days you can drag and drop on a computer, but he would precisely and manually cut and paste. Raju would say, 'This is real editing.' He was happy to be doing something creative. 'Normally we don't touch raga alapanas while editing. We just cut the apaswara notes out. But here you are asking me to shuffle the notes around!' It was almost like we were producing the raga using what we had, and it was very exciting when you pulled something like this off and it sounded good. Those were some very beautiful days.

After this, I sang for a number of companies. Always for a meagre fixed amount and no royalties. HMV was the only exception. I still receive some royalty from them, even if it's a small amount.

I had an interesting experience with the INRECO label. They released two albums that were recordings from my Australian tour of 1995. That double volume was titled 'Live Waves from Melbourne'. Initially, they weren't convinced that it would be a good idea to release a single Ragam Tanam Pallavi from the concert as an album CD. But I stood my ground, insisting that classical music be presented in the manner it deserves to be. We broke some unwritten rules with this album. Back then, all labels carried at least twelve to fourteen songs in hour-long Carnatic CDs. The main piece would last up to twenty minutes, and the other songs just four minutes each. I wanted to break away from these restrictions, insisting that I would sing at least one song for half an hour.

Following these experiments, I even ventured into album production briefly in 1997 with a label called Sahana Sounds. Our first production was a solo album of violinist R.K. Shriram Kumar. We still have the DAT tapes for the album and the stickers for the cassettes. Aarthi would do all the marketing, carrying the cassettes to Saraswati Stores every month and looking into collecting the payments. I remember going to the Landmark store in Chennai to meet Jai Subramaniam. I told them that they should play Carnatic music; that's when people will hear it and buy it. The store's response was that they did play it every day. I asked, 'When?' Pat came the answer, 'Morning. 8.30, as soon as we open the store!' I said, 'Nobody is in the store then. Who will listen to the songs?' Finally, that day, they played my CD. Immediately, every single staff member looked up at the guy in charge of the music and motioned to him in an irate manner to turn it off. They'd been conditioned to think that this music could be played only in the morning as a prayer when nobody was there in the store.

It was during this time that I finally found the space I was looking for. In 1997, the recording label Charsur was founded. The record company said, 'Why are you getting into the nitty-gritties of selling? You sing, we will produce.' My association with the label was very warm because they wanted to make quality products. They wanted to produce Carnatic music but didn't care about following market dynamics. So, they were happy with any new concept I took to them. I came up with the idea of 'one, two, three, four' for them. One: full RTP as an album. Two: Dvayam, a study of the two ragas Kambhoji and Ritigowla. Three: the album *The Magic of the Trinity*, with a Thyagaraja song ('Manasa Etulo'), a Deekshitar composition ('Geeti Chakra') and one Syama Sastri krithi ('Palintsau Kamakshi'), each in a different raga, Malayamarutam, Kannada and Madhyamavati. Four: the album *Chathushram*, with four songs, one in Tamizh, Harikesanallur Muthiah Bhagavathar's 'Aarukum Adangatha Neeli' in Begada, 'Palukute' by Annamacharya in Telugu set in Abheri, Purandara Dasa's Kannada composition 'Hari Vasaradha' in Sindhubhairavi and in Malayalam Swati Thirunal's 'Jagadeesha' in Nattaikurunji. This album released in 2006, marking fifty years of the reorganisation of the southern states along linguistic lines.

Going to studios back then was a fun experience, especially being around for those early days of computer editing. These discs had phenomenal reach, I realised, because listeners at my concerts would request songs they'd heard on CDs or they would come to my concert for the first time having heard a recording. Charsur's top two albums back then were Bombay Jayashree's. Mine was third. I recorded with them almost exclusively for fifteen years. We also released a number of studio recordings and many live concert CDs, including a full December season pack that had fourteen CDs from seven concerts.

It so happened that this time that I was recording for Charsur was also when I was working with the Tamil language and its musicality. I was finally able to make the leap to better articulation of the texts musically. For instance, my rendition of a song that recounts the story of the nayanmar (Shaivite bhakti saint) Nandanar, 'Vazhi Maraittirukkude', had actually evolved so much during this period that I even experimented while singing it on stage. I used every line of the song as a neraval (improv) take-off point to the pallavi refrain, which is about the Lord not being visible to the 'outcast'. It is a beautifully articulated sentiment, and so many lines of the lament make sense in its entirety to the central theme of the composition, which recounts the instance of the saint, born in a so-called untouchable caste, being denied entry to the temple. For instance, the song features Nandanar saying, 'It is enough if I stand near the temple car and look at the Lord,' and of course this has a direct relationship to the pallavi where a bull blocks his view.

In the eighties, Rukmini paati had sung the song along with a group she led at the Academy morning session. It was a forum where her husband, my granduncle T.V. Rajagopalan, a lawyer and a music-enthusiast, was delivering a presentation on Gopalakrishna Bharati's magnum opus *Nandanar Charitiram*, which recounts the saint's life. In fact, it was TVR who first suggested removing the word 'Parayan' and replacing it with 'Nandan'—after all, the references in those songs were to him. I was exposed to the politics of this reference, which was also used by the so-called upper castes as a casteist slur, only much later, in the nineties, and have since adopted the same for other songs of his too.

For about a decade after this, I recorded albums regularly, but by the mid-2000s, I'd had enough and finally put an end to my studio visits. Doing just live concert CDs seemed to be enough. Something just didn't work anymore, and I was getting angrier with the process itself. I began to find the whole thing inorganic—the editing, voice mixing, singing the same lines over and over and correcting pitch using software. It all began to feel very artificial. There's no doubt the final product did well, but I had begun to go off the studio atmosphere. What had changed? As the years rolled on, being in the studio began to make me feel inadequate, especially about my voice.

The recording studio throws up your inefficiencies, highlights and magnifies them. This same fear is probably what held me back from singing in films too, even after my rigid notions of what was an acceptable soundscape for me to participate in had begun to dissipate. I wasn't able to do even Carnatic very well in studios, even though this music was my comfort zone. In film music, they do things very differently. Would my voice even suit all that? I think, in hindsight, those fears were just as big a factor in my mind as my principled stand on wanting to sing only Carnatic music back then.

In the midst of all this, I had also gone into business with Charsur, setting up an exclusive showroom for Carnatic products and their CDs. It eventually went bust, and I ended up losing money, but it was good fun while it lasted. I don't blame anyone, I just wasn't smart enough to see what was coming.

This exciting era ended once music entered the digital space. Everything changed. There was too much music available online, and you could no longer make any money selling CDs.

So long as I was working with companies, and there was robust physical distribution of CDs, I did make some money from records. Not a lot, but that was because of my own principles. I was never commercially savvy because I wanted to be musically strong. I never agreed to sing a devotional album or just tukdas, for instance, which would have been lucrative. If I wanted it to be a source of revenue, I could have sung eight or ten albums a year, but I did only two purely classical albums a year.

Records were always a numbers game. Balamurali sang a hundred albums for Sangeetha, as did the Bombay Sisters. Unni too recorded an impressive number. I, personally, never experienced that high from numbers. For me, the high lay in singing concerts.

I sang 120 concerts in a year because live performances were what charged me up.

Eventually, I stopped recording albums, lost touch with that process and ecosystem and soon forgot what the experience of singing in a studio was even like, until my recent collaborations with Sean Roldan and Ilaiyaraja.

During those recording years, legendary Tamil film music director M.S. Viswanathan (MSV) was producing a series called *Aathmadarshini* for Doordarshan. He asked KSK maama if I would sing the title song, who in turn asked me to go do it. I went to AVM Studios at 7 a.m. one day and was there for twelve hours. He didn't look at me even once. A video was playing, and he was composing the background score. At 7.15 p.m., he asked, 'Who's singing the title song?' His assistant pointed to me. I sang about three lines for thirty seconds. Then I had to sing two lines of pallavi of the song *Ardhanareeswaram*. I didn't sing for more than twenty minutes in all. It didn't occur to me through the whole day, and I blame my age for this now, to just go and greet MSV. I sat there quietly, sang and came home. I think now about all the things I would have loved to discuss with him, if only I could.

When I was finally ready to branch out and broached the topic with Sean Roldan, he recorded a song with me—an Akkamahadevi vachana, 'Bettada Melondu'—and mixed it with an electronic dance music track. He sent it to me with trepidation and said, 'Please don't take this the wrong way.' He was worried that I'd think it blasphemous to listen to such fusion. His wife, the singer Lalitha Sudha, was terrified and scolded him. But I told them both not to worry, that this was exactly the kind of experiment I was opening myself up to.

Everyone who heard it with me loved it. I also liked the way my voice sounded, so I knew there was something here that we could work with. When we were in the middle of this, I sang my first playback track for him, 'Yedhudhaan Ingu Sandhosam', for the film *Lucky Man*. Sean, who was the music director of the film, is brilliant. He eased me into these new directions.

For my part, I did my homework when I went to sing for him. I gathered all his work from the last ten years, heard it ten times, made a playlist of it. I had to enter that mindset. I didn't want to just say, 'I am a Carnatic musician, I'll sing what I want.' As far as this space was concerned, I was a novice. My intention was to learn and to work with him.

As my former student, Sean was as loving as he was supportive. He said, 'Anna, we have to be careful. I can't just have you sing anything. You've been working so hard, singing for so long. I can't let a thing I do break your reputation.' He is meticulous in his work. He pays close attention to the sound and quality of the voice as he records, and his hard work and precision are evident in the final product. Technology plays a big role, transforming how music is recorded and produced today. But the successful artists still follow the same basic principles—hard work, attention to detail, high creative ability and a solid grasp of aesthetics.

Later, when I came up with the idea of an album of Vallalar arutpa songs, Vignesh Sundaresan and the Onemai Foundation funded the whole project as an art commission (something unheard of in our part of the world), and I was given the choice of working with anyone. I asked Sean if he would come on board, and he immediately agreed. In fact, he suggested that we form a band to make this album. I liked the fact that apart from being a musician, he also knows how to think like a music producer. In India, if you are a music producer, you are also a composer and you usually work in films. In non-film musical albums, the lead singer doubles up as the producer. I felt that I was not competent to call myself a producer for *Anbenum Peruveli*. Sean, who'd produced indie albums with his band, Sean Roldan & Friends, could fill that role.

To begin with, Vikram Vivekanand on guitar, Shalini Mohan on bass, Ramkumar Kanakarajan on drums, Sean and I jammed for two days as we worked on six songs for the album. During these two days, we created a framework for all the songs, decided how we would go about recording, what kind of loops we would keep, etc. Then we booked a studio where we recorded only the instruments. We fixed the basic band structure and recorded that. Watching this unfold was an educative experience. How they worked as a band, with the sounds, with music, chords. Finally, Sean mixed my voice, after which he worked with Kalyani Nair for the strings as well as the chorus for which he wrote the music. The Celtic Folk Ensemble recorded the string section at London's iconic Abbey Road Studios for this album.

In the midst of all this, for season two of Coke Studio Tamil, Sean introduced me to Girish Gopalakrishnan, who too comes from a Carnatic background. I didn't know what I was going to sing, and when I went in to record the song 'Elay Makka', it was completely different from anything I had done until then. He asked if I was okay with the song, and I reassured him, 'I am ready to sing anything!' Given how well all of these songs have been received, my sense is that the audience has quickly warmed up to me moving into these spaces.

❖

Why did I return to the studios in this avatar, and not remain a purely Carnatic musician at this stage of my career? This is a question I have been constantly asked of late. After much soul searching, my answer is this: a combination of frustration and my need to move on. Not frustration with the music, but with the system. When the pandemic came, it became obvious that this huge system that you thought would back you did not care that much about you. Even after the pandemic, I don't think the audience has come back to the sabhas in the old numbers. There are just not enough people invested in the Carnatic music system to give it that boost because it doesn't make overall economic sense.

But that's only one part of the story. Most importantly, I was ready to move on. The pandemic years brought home the realisation that I still had some years ahead of me. I am a very young fifty-five-year-old, in that sense. So, I was ready to open myself up to trying something new. We are living longer these days, and one has to be productive. To be productive, one needs to keep moving on to new things. This is also why I am learning to play the piano now.

During the making of *Anbenum Peruveli,* the rest of the band communicated with each other only in chords. They were all about the A, G, C and D ... and I just never got the hang of it. At first I just thought, 'Where will I go now and learn about all this?' But then, all through that process, I felt left out. I began to wonder if I should buy myself a keyboard then.

I'll be honest, I hated keyboards mainly because of their inability to reproduce gamakams, but these days I have trained myself to think beyond my Carnatic roots. I ask myself, if you were a singer, what could you do with a keyboard? An important moment in this journey came when I met Ilaiyaraja (or Raja as us fans call him) earlier this year. He played something for me, and then graciously offered his keyboard to me and asked if I wanted to play. I sheepishly admitted that I couldn't. I felt silly then. What was I doing? Intending to right the wrong immediately, I went and bought a digital piano (rather than a keyboard) to explore the fundamentals. Even the most basic concepts, like the structure of an octave, were revelations to me. Somehow, these details, that five black keys and seven white keys make up an octave, had never occupied my mind. My daughter teased me: 'Oh, you bought a keyboard now because you've met Ilaiyaraja, is it?' In reality, the events of the last few years were building up to me spending time on a piano, and meeting the maestro was just the catalyst I needed.

I have been a fan of Ilaiyaraja's music from a young age—after all, we grew up to his soundtrack. When I met him recently, I told him about collecting lyric pamphlets of the films he scored for, and that I used to have booklets from almost 150 films in the early eighties. But as I became more serious about my Carnatic music practice, I distanced myself from film songs. Of course it's impossible to live in Chennai and not encounter the music of its cinema. So, I occasionally did hear Ilaiyaraja songs, while watching films, at the gym or on music channels. My children too played whatever was popular at the time, but I didn't have the leisure to listen to music as intently as I did during Raja's heyday or the early years of A.R. Rahman. Five years ago, I had received a call from Raja asking me to record a devotional song. At the time, I declined.

After going through a shift in my thinking and gaining confidence from singing playback for Sean, I decided recently that it was time for me to approach Raja. *I am in that space where I can go and see him,* I thought. When he had called me earlier, I think there was this egoistic notion I had that he should first listen to my concert and only then could I sing for him. The silliness of that notion makes me smile now. I made up my mind to go see him whenever my first film song came out. But that was delayed, as things around films tend to be, and the song was released only in August 2023. I had to go on a tour right after that, and the music season started when I got back.

In the meantime, I had done a series of videos on my YouTube channel called Short Notes, where I explored a raga and ended always on a note from a popular Raja song set in that raga. At a concert in KK Nagar, sometime in the late nineties, I was singing an alapana of abhogi, and as I finished it I sang a slow phrase—sa dha ma ga ri sa—keeping in mind the Ilaiyaraja classic 'Kaalai

Nera Poonguyil'. K. Arun Prakash, the mridangam artist and a Raja pundit, threw me an expression that I've never quite got over. I almost burst out laughing on stage then. On that day, the seeds of what would become Short Notes were sowed.

When Varadarajan went to accompany TVG for a concert in Raja's house after I started my series, Raja reportedly said to Varadu, 'What pa your friend is singing "On that note", is it? It's good. I did it a certain way, he's doing it in a different way.' This was just the acknowledgment of my existence and my music that I needed from him. Then, at Ranjini Gayathri's 'Raja by RaGa' event, he referred to my 'On that Note' again, and I couldn't wait to see him.

When Aarthi and I finally visited him at his home, it turned out to be a magical four hours. He spoke to me with such kindness, mentioning songs of mine that he had heard. I shared with him my work on Vallalar and sang a few songs. He listened intently, clearly pleased. Then, he took us to the room where he composes his music and even played some of his songs. He said that he typically takes about half an hour to compose a song, with the beautiful 'Padu Nilave' being the one exception that took longer. When he sang for us finally, I was mesmerised. For about a minute afterwards, I was completely speechless. He asked us if we were in a hurry to leave, and Aarthi joked that we would not leave until he threw us out.

'How can you say I'd do something like that?' he chided. 'There is this re-recording going on. Would you like to watch?' We, of course, said yes.

In the recording room, he sat at the keyboard. The engineer, Aarthi, a friend of ours and I joined him. He worked for an hour, and then reached a point in the film where there was a song.

He looked at me then, and asked me to sing four lines. 'Let this be the beginning!' he added.

He taught me the lines right away, and I learnt the song.

Then he took his phone out and said, 'First I'll record in this, we can go ahead when the director okays it.'

Twenty minutes after he recorded my voice, the director of the film, Vetri Maaran, walked in. Raja introduced us and told him that he had recorded a song with me. The director readily agreed to feature my voice. Raja then asked me to go see Napoleon in the next room to record the song.

Napoleon asked briskly, 'Are you the singer?'

Here was another legend, I was a fan of his, and he had no clue who I was. I recorded the song and went home without thinking much of it. That night, I messaged to ask if I could share my photograph with him on social media, and Raja agreed. I put up my photo with him with the message 'Greatest moment of our lives'. This is how I came to sing my first song for Ilaiyaraja, for the film *Viduthalai 2*.

At that first meeting, Ilaiyaraja had insisted that he wanted to record a longer, full song with me. Since *Viduthalai 2* had already released at the Rotterdam festival, I figured it would be for a future film project. I even googled what his upcoming films were to figure out what I might be lending my voice to.

Soon enough, I got a call.

As I waited to meet Ilaiyaraja outside his studio, Vetri Maaran came out of the room and said, 'Come in, sir is calling you.'

This time, Vetri Maaran took out a camera and began recording the 'making' video.

Raja said, 'Come, come. They've already placed the song you sang in the film. Now they're going to shoot a new song before the release in India. We're going to record now.' Ilaiyaraja had written the lyrics himself.

He started to teach me the song in his studio. For about twenty minutes, he taught it to me line by line. 'Slowly, you must come off into our world,' he said as he taught me the song.

At first, I found it a bit difficult to pick up the nuances. He was very clear about what he wanted. When I didn't get a line, he taught it to me 200 times. (I am not even exaggerating, it really was 200 times.) In this relationship, he is the teacher and I am the student. It is important here that our minds meet, and I give him what he wants. I have seen this process unfold as both a student and as a teacher—what is sung may be 'correct', but it may not be what the teacher had on his mind. At times, Raja wanted me to incorporate a little bit of breathiness in my voice in a line. Or he wanted a particular kind of glide in a phrase. And when I got that glide, I may have missed the emotion of the lyric or the pronunciation. Recording, in that sense, is like miniature painting. Every detail must be just so, because you are creating a record for all time to come. It is not like the live concerts that I am used to, where I try many ideas in one concert and immediately move on to the next one. And in that recording space, Raja is the master, he has been doing it for so long.

We went through this entire process with no sign of irritation (on either side) because we were clear about this relationship of teacher and student. He kept teaching, and I kept singing. It went on and on. Until I got it, he taught it. We never lost sight of the fact that we were working together to create something. When you reach that place, the number of repetitions needed to get something right is immaterial.

When he came to the last line, he warned me, 'This one line is a bit musical. You'll be able to sing the rest fine.' I found the line fascinating. I fixed a scale from it and told him, 'This can be a raga by itself.' I sang swaram, and he played along. It was a lovely musical exchange. By the end of it, he'd already created a new song. Between the time I had an idea and explained it to him, not only had he picked it up, he had very nearly created another song out of it. That's Ilaiyaraja for you.

He even recorded the song on my phone in his voice, had me listen to it fully and went out. When he returned, Raja didn't approve of what I had recorded: 'Let's just do it once more.'

The way I had used my voice was not working for him. Apart from the actual musical phrase and the song, he also had a particular tone in mind that he wanted me to convey. Eventually, he made me change the very way I sing.

The opening line of the first song I sang for Raja was about the first meeting between two people, and he asked me to sing it smiling. He even gestured to Aarthi and said, 'When did you meet her first, and how did you smile then?' It was a song in the folk genre, and he taught it to me with such warmth and love.

As we were recording, he added, 'This one line which is about someone being troubled will look a bit troublesome, but don't worry, you'll sing it.'

I told him, 'I am reminded of my days with SRD sir. I went to him to learn a keerthanam after singing concerts for twenty years. He made me sit there for two and a half hours. This feels exactly like that.' He was elated with that comparison. I ended up recording four different songs with him in a matter of months after this, and each experience was just as exhilarating. And in true cinematic fashion, which of those songs will make it to the final film will remain a mystery, at least for a while.

Back when I was entrenched in the bias and conditioning of the Carnatic tradition, I believed that I was the king of my domain. Today, I approach these musical spaces with a childlike sense of wonder. I want to experience everything, do everything, try everything.

CHAPTER 8

Partners in Time

Speaking of fulfilling partnerships and collaborators in life and art, I must pause to tell you about Aarthi. Her family and mine have known each other for many years. She was also my brother's classmate. We'd met through common friends when she was just eighteen and had long conversations on the phone. We talked a lot back then—we were in the same milieu and apparently had things to say. For me, it was thrilling to have a woman companion, because I came from a household where such interactions were rare. I was so caught up in my music that I wasn't even looking for such a companion, except as any man that age might consider such a prospect.

She was remarkably sorted, and would discuss books passionately. My conversations with girls until then had stayed in the realm of music, about Bhairavi, Shankarabharanam and raga intricacies at best. But Aarthi brought into my social life something that was conspicuously missing: intellectual stimulation. We liked each other very much, but it is this quality that led us close to one another.

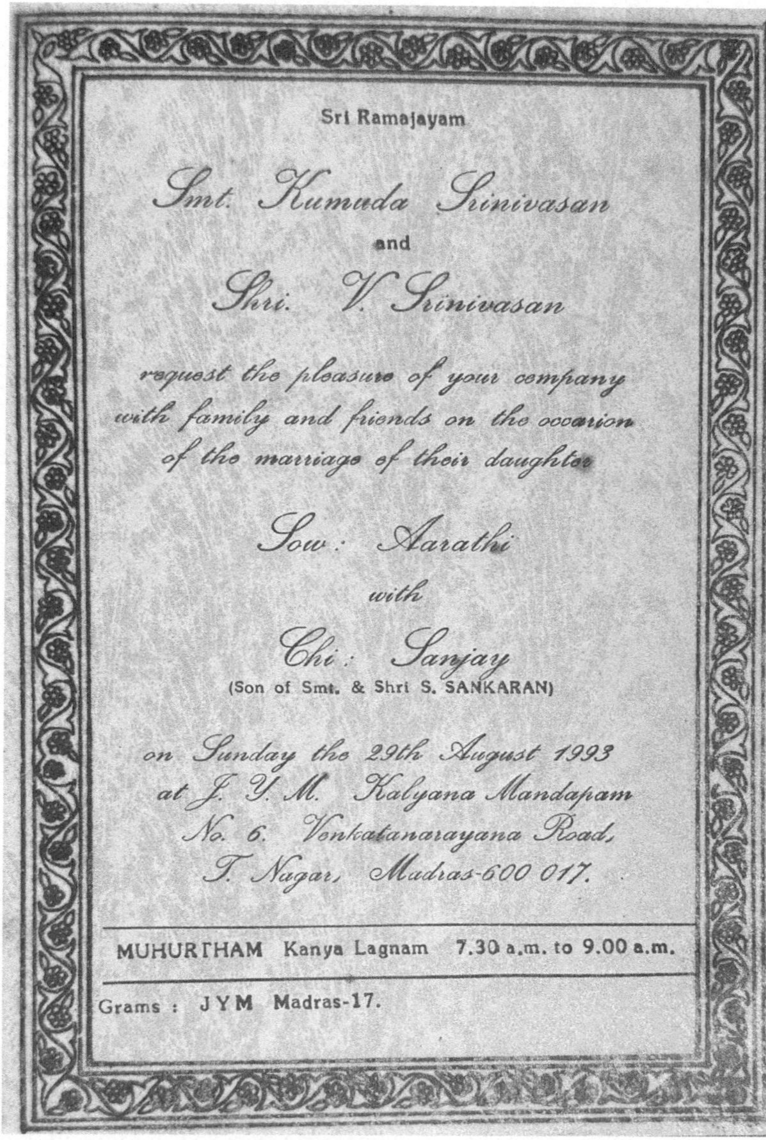

Sri Ramajayam

Smt. Kumuda Srinivasan

and

Shri. V. Srinivasan

request the pleasure of your company with family and friends on the occasion of the marriage of their daughter

Sow: Aarathi

with

Chi: Sanjay

(Son of Smt. & Shri S. SANKARAN)

on Sunday the 29th August 1993
at J. Y. M. Kalyana Mandapam
No. 6. Venkatanarayana Road,
T. Nagar, Madras-600 017.

MUHURTHAM Kanya Lagnam 7.30 a.m. to 9.00 a.m.

Grams : JYM Madras-17.

Our wedding invitation

One day, I asked her if she would marry me, and she said, 'Absolutely.' Then immediately, everything changed—now that it was official that we were in love, we had to get married, and quickly. So much has changed now. The two of us often talk about those days now and wonder what it would have been like if this love story had unfolded today. When Aarthi turned twenty, it was simply understood that she had to get married. There wasn't an option, like the one we want our children to have. The freedom of choice. To say, 'If you find someone and want to get married, do it, but if you don't want to, that's fine too. There's no pressure.'

Aarthi might have pursued her master's degree had she not got married. Instead, she decided to go through Montessori training and then started working. That too lasted only a year, in great part due to my crazy travel schedule.

Through the whole period of our courtship though, my music was the last thing on our minds. Until after our wedding, we never spoke about my singing at all. She had come for a concert or two, but for that whole year, we had other things to talk to each other: life, philosophy, anything and everything but music.

Interestingly enough, once we decided to marry, things changed. She started to come to my kutcheris, and would point out to me that this song or that phrase was good. The fact that she had learnt music helped too. She watched out for me, and her concerns would come through in our conversations. I recall once, when I sang a navavarnam in Sastry Hall, she said that the first line of the charanam was very moving. When I told a musical friend about it, he said, 'Hey, she's got good musical knowledge.' I felt validated when I heard these things about her too. Back then, it was common to hear stories of relationships going bad where one person was a musician and the other wasn't. There was even that famous movie *Pudhu Pudhu Arthangal* about this very thing.

With us, it was evidently different. After the marriage, Aarthi was fully invested in my music. Until my daughter was born in 1996, we would travel together on tours, and she would play the tambura on these travels. We got married ahead of a tour in Malaysia. It felt like a lifetime of holiday stretched ahead of us in those early days when we were travelling constantly. It was an exciting couple of years.

Aarthi would come to my kutcheris, play tambura and would even tell me what I could learn next. She would hear some recording and insist I sing the song. It was not that I didn't know the song or that, because she found it, I had to sing it. She would have a convincing reason for why I had to sing it. It was always something specific, either about the song or the way it was sung.

One time, I was at the Landmark bookstore to buy *Calvin and Hobbes* when I chanced upon an M.S. Subbulakshmi tape. It had the Syama Shastri krithi 'Devi Brova Samaymide'. I remember her telling me, 'How beautifully she's sung this song, line after

Aarthi on the tambura at a concert

line. This is what a keerthanam should sound like.' These were the very values I wanted to embody in my own singing. The fact that someone close to me, someone who genuinely cared about my growth, was urging me to internalise these ideals had an impact on me. This kind of advice felt different from what teachers or fans would give me. It was more personal, more invested, devoid of criticism. It came from a place of security and deep affection. It took me years to fully grasp this nuance. But there was always love, which led me to trust her ideas implicitly, without having to resort to rationalising.

Of course, there were also songs I sang that she didn't like. She'd make her disapproval known, and I'd snap back, 'What do you even know?' This kind of banter often led to one of two outcomes: either the song would eventually lose its appeal for me, or she'd come to appreciate it over time.

She also hated it when I sang with the door closed at home; she wanted to hear the music even when I was just practising. For the first decade or so, she learnt everything I was singing just by listening. I would be teaching students a song, and if I forgot a sangathi, she would come in and remind me. She actively contributed to my music until the children came along.

If I said something in public that she didn't agree with, she would tell me right away. Until I met Aarthi, I didn't care much for anyone's opinion. But she quickly became my inbuilt editor, shaping my thoughts and words.

As I've said before, I've always had a problem with my voice, but she has always held that it is my strong suit. So high is my esteem of her opinion that, even at my lowest, this would do wonders for me.

Our family cultures were radically different, even if both Aarthi and I were raised on middle class values. For instance, I had a cot for the first time in my life when I got married, and she had never slept on the floor until after marriage! We weren't living in luxury either; it was all train or bus travel, making do with what we had. If I didn't have enough concerts in a month, I'd go ask Appa for Rs 2,000 or 5,000. 'What is this, da,' he would scold. So I started sending her to get the money from him. Once, I bought an air conditioner for Rs 29,000. I sent her to get the cheque from my father, having already spoken to him. The disapproval was palpable in his every gesture, she came back and said. I reasoned that we didn't have to suffer through the oppressive Chennai summer when he could help us.

My parents-in-law have been among my earliest and staunchest supporters. They were regular attendees of my concerts, and keen music enthusiasts boasting an impressive collection of recordings. Once I married their daughter, their collection became exclusively dedicated to one artist.

Aravind, my brother-in-law, is a cricket coach, and was my junior in school, which helped foster a close, informal relationship. I have accompanied him on his matches for Alwarpet CC, where many cricketers have heard my concerts on their Walkmans and, later, mp3 players. His wife Bharathi and their daughter Rachna too are keen listeners. I have it on good authority that Aravind has forced them to listen to my concerts, rewinding and playing his personal highlights many times. Today, they are some of my first listeners, especially when I record something new.

At some point, after we had children, Aarthi and I looked up and, just like that, fifteen years had flown by. We jokingly ask each other now, what happened to those fifteen years? Whatever happened between the ages of thirty and forty-five? Children take over your concerns once they arrive, and so we had decided to wait a few years to have children.

Eventually, our first-born, Shreyasi, arrived, and it changed me fundamentally as a person. When she was almost four, our son Sushanth was born. In hindsight, the conversations Aarthi and I used to have about major life decisions bordered on silly. 'Hey I am X age now, by the time I am fifty, I would like my child to be Y age ...' These were the kinds of ideas we had. We were both strong, but we also learnt to go with the flow. We learnt to be carefree, and this nonchalance allowed us to navigate life without feeling its strain. Happily for us, both Shreyasi and Sushanth were the kind of kids parents dream of. Throughout my whirlwind travel schedule during their formative years, they were supportive. They were regulars at my Chennai concerts, a presence I deeply valued. Both are incredibly artistic, each responding to the world in their unique way. Today, they've carved out careers that align with their passions, finding joy in both their professional and social circles.

They are both attuned to music, in a different way, though. They learnt formally only occasionally, but they would come for all my concerts.

Shreyasi's response to my concerts has always been very emotional. Even as a child, she would cry when she heard some ragas in my concerts. On some days, when she came home from school, I might be singing a raga that tended to upset her. She would mutter to herself, 'What on earth is happening in this house!' And because she would cry to one particular raga, Sushanth would pick a different raga and say, 'Only if you sing this song, I would feel like crying!' It became a running joke soon enough. All of us would look at Shreyasi when I sang Kaapi in a concert, and on cue she would start wailing uncontrollably. It's actually a trait she's inherited from Aarthi and her mother. It's how they all listen. Even some musical phrases affect them.

I am sure the kids have their own version of those years, but back then, all of our lives seemed to revolve around my concerts. I remember Shreyasi was about eleven, and she had her Maths exam the next day when I had to sing a primetime concert at Vani Mahal. At 7 p.m., she signalled to me and said, 'No RTP. Come, I have to study for my exam!' She kept gesturing to me vigorously, demanding I stop the concert. If you want to not have any airs about being an artist, have children. They will bring you down to earth. When my son was about seven, he discovered Michael Jackson, and asked Aarthi who according to her was the greatest singer in the world. When she said, 'Appa da', he said to her, 'I asked about the greatest! He's a local singer.' Shreyasi once came to a concert, and right there asked Aarthi with her trademark sarcasm, 'What, your husband can't fill Narada Gana Sabha, is it?'

We both joke now that our kids are what they are in spite of us, and not because of us. We were not as aware back then—how I wish we had the chance to do it all over again with all the maturity and experience we have now! Honestly, we thought we were doing a fantastic job. Today I'm willing to accept that I was wrong and tell them, 'You guys did well. And we're sorry if we didn't make it as smooth as we should have for you.'

In fact, as Aarthi and I grow older, our children teach us a lot. I often ask Sushanth if it's okay to phrase something a certain way, and he'll explain, 'Don't say it like this; say it that way.' We've become more sensitive and are constantly learning from them. We never dismiss their advice, and that has come to be the foundation of the healthy relationship we have with them now. I think it is because of my relationship with Shreyasi and Sushanth that I am able to pull off something like appearing on Coke Studio, where I have to follow the lead of Sean and Girish who are so much younger than me.

Those years, when the kids were growing up were a blur indeed, but a lot was going on. I took some financial risks during that time. Between 2003 and 2006, I sang 140 concerts each year. However, from 2006 to 2009, I scaled back to ninety concerts annually.

I began to turn down concerts where I wasn't given a chance to negotiate my pay. It was time for a pushback. By my late thirties, as the feeling of monotony began to set in, I needed to cut back on the number of concerts I performed, and the only way I could do that was to increase my remuneration.

When we discussed what I should charge, Aarthi would say, 'You are worth more.' I could never bring myself to agree with her. I'd say, 'Look at Bombay Jayashree, Unnikrishnan and Nithyashree. Look at the crowds they are pulling. Am I getting that crowd? How can I ask what they are asking?' She saw it differently: 'For the concert organisers, you're all the same.' Her clarity was my supply of confidence and courage. Over the years, together we began to trust that, whatever the logical next level might be, I would get there.

As I approached fifty, with the kids both in college and our loans nearly paid off, I thought I could finally settle into a new phase in my musical career. Then, out of the blue, the Sangita Kalanidhi came. Leading up to the award, everything had begun to snowball and move at a dizzying pace. The years preceding it, from 2011 until 2014, had been a period of real highs. With the kids becoming more independent, both Aarthi and I found ourselves freer, and that freedom definitely reflected in my music. I was in a much more relaxed space, both personally and musically, exploring new creative paths.

Throughout those years of creative exploration, historian and author V. Sriram too had a significant influence on me. Together, we started *sangeetham.com*, which stoked my passion for research further. Sharada, a chartered accountant-turned-entrepreneur (and Sriram's wife), was the driving force behind this venture. She even lined up potential venture funds (but I think we missed the bus by a few months since the dot-com bubble had already begun to burst).

Until then, I enjoyed data, history and biographies, but I hadn't seriously engaged in analytical research. Sriram's influence led me to delve deeply into the subjects I was singing about. Once I started reading extensively, I found myself with a wealth of new content at my disposal. New ideas began to emerge from the research material, allowing me to venture out of my comfort zone.

V.K. Shankar, a very good friend, was impressed with the work we were doing on *sangeetham.com*. He invited us to visit him and opened up his personal archives to us. Among his treasures were notations of tunes written by his grandfather, V.S. Gomathisankara Iyer, a brilliant archivist who spent fifty years at Annamalai University. This access to such rare and valuable material opened more doors for us, and took me further in my constant search for information and inspiration.

When I started out as a musician, I had aimed to be a pure Carnatic singer with a very clear and defined aesthetic framework in my mind. I almost set boundaries for myself, insisting that my creativity should flourish within it. Surprisingly, despite these self-imposed boundaries, I occasionally found myself making unexpected detours. I'd sing a raga or a swara that seemed out of tune with my strict ideals. Accompanying artists asked, 'How come you're singing this raga?' To such a question I had no concrete answers. A creative thought would appear from somewhere, and I'd follow its lead.

While it's often hard to pinpoint exactly where an idea emerged from, I can trace the origins of some of these detours. In the early 2000s, I began integrating elements from Hindustani music into my performances. Similarly, encountering Pakistani classical music inspired me to incorporate its nuances. I've even tried to capture the essence of rock and jazz in my swaras sometimes. Musical triggers continue to come and go as I journey through life.

Aarthi too has been a significant influence on some creative choices, especially with respect to lyrics. When I listen to a song, I primarily absorb its music—the rhythm, the sound. But Aarthi hears the words and influences how I use them. She'd suggest, 'This line is good; why don't you sing this as a virutham?'

CHAPTER 9

A Wandering Musician

It is a fact universally acknowledged that, in the life of a musician, there's never a dearth of adventures or stories. It's also a fact that I've got in all kinds of trouble for telling some stories as they happened!

Back in the nineties, for instance, whenever we went to the US to perform, a sequence of events would unfold. Sometimes it still does.

We were usually hosted by NRIs, and they'd even graciously come to pick us up. The first thing they would do was ask, shocked, 'So much luggage?' And on seeing the mridangam, they'd ask, 'Has it come without any damage?' Of course they were asking out of concern, but the poor mridangist was anxious about the instrument to begin with, and the question would only make things worse. After these pleasantries, we'd all get in the car. The hosts would be pretty nervous until they had paid the parking fee and crossed the exit gates. They'd always have doubts about which exit gate to use, especially in the pre-Google Maps days. They'd only relax when they had finally made their way on to the highway. The very next word from them would be 'So?' And someone in the vehicle would invariably ask, 'Is this your first trip to the US?' Every time.

We usually have a pool running to see which of us might escape this question. On the last day of one such trip, Varadu told me he lost: 'Ayyo, no one asked until today; they finally did, Sanjay!'

Then a barrage of questions, the same each time, no matter which city or what occasion.

Where was your last concert?

Where are you going for the next concert?

How many concerts have you performed in all?

How do you take care of your voice?

Is it not affected by the weather?

Do you take any precautions for your voice's safety?

Do you have any diet restrictions?

Have you visited this place before?

Even those who've known you and are seeing you after a while will run through this standard set. The accompanists usually sit in the back, and I have to sit in the front seat and tackle the questions.

Once the concert is over, the hosts usually organise a dinner with a bunch of guests. And once again these questions will make the rounds, in pretty much the same sequence. This second time, I slink to a corner and leave the accompanists to face the volley, which might even include personal details like their marital status. During my first tour of Toronto, Aarthi was twenty-two and I was twenty-seven. The hosts didn't realise we were married, and thought she had just come to play the tambura. They even called her aside and asked her, 'You just go with him wherever like this, is it?'

I wrote about all this on *sangeetham.com*, back when we were running it and added that I would like to have a questionnaire before my next trip, so I can readily prepare the answers and hand it out to those I run into. A lot of people laughed it off, but then I received a very strong reply from a lady in the US, who said, 'How dare you write like this? We make so many sacrifices; we give up our bedrooms for artists who come to our house; we cook for three to four days; we host them. They ask us to do this and that. We are at their beck and call, but you make fun of us like this?'

Of course, they must have hosted some difficult artists. I've heard of people who would demand chapathis at 4 p.m. and threaten the hosts that they would not sing if their demands weren't met. In my defence, back when we were young, we were often offered the hosts' child's room and their children's tiny bed. We got used to it all, however. We were not the kind to make demands, and it was fun too, I cannot deny that. Our hosts also took good care of us. They'd take us around, drive us out to shop. And we made the most of it.

As a singer, travel can be both an occupational hazard and an adventure. Once, while going to the US, I was waiting to get my visa stamped. This one officer asked me, 'What do you play?' I said, 'I sing.' Why don't you sing for me, he asked, and I sang a small raaga phrase in Todi for him. 'Why don't you sing something with words?' So I sang 'Kaddanuvariki'. I was a bit worried he would ask for the meaning, and I had no idea what the words meant. But he said okay, and let me in.

When I married Aarthi, I promised her that I wouldn't travel more than ten days a month. However, within a few years, I found myself on tours to the US lasting three and a half months. I've now accumulated seven passports and made about seventy-three trips just for concerts in the last three decades.

Right after our wedding, in the year 1993, Aarthi and I travelled to Singapore, Malaysia and Indonesia on a concert tour. We got married on 29 August, and left home in less than a fortnight, on 12 September. My friends in Malaysia had arranged the tour. I was going to perform four concerts in a single venue over a period of ten days, with different sponsors for each day. About 200 people attended, and it turned out to be a very good tour for me.

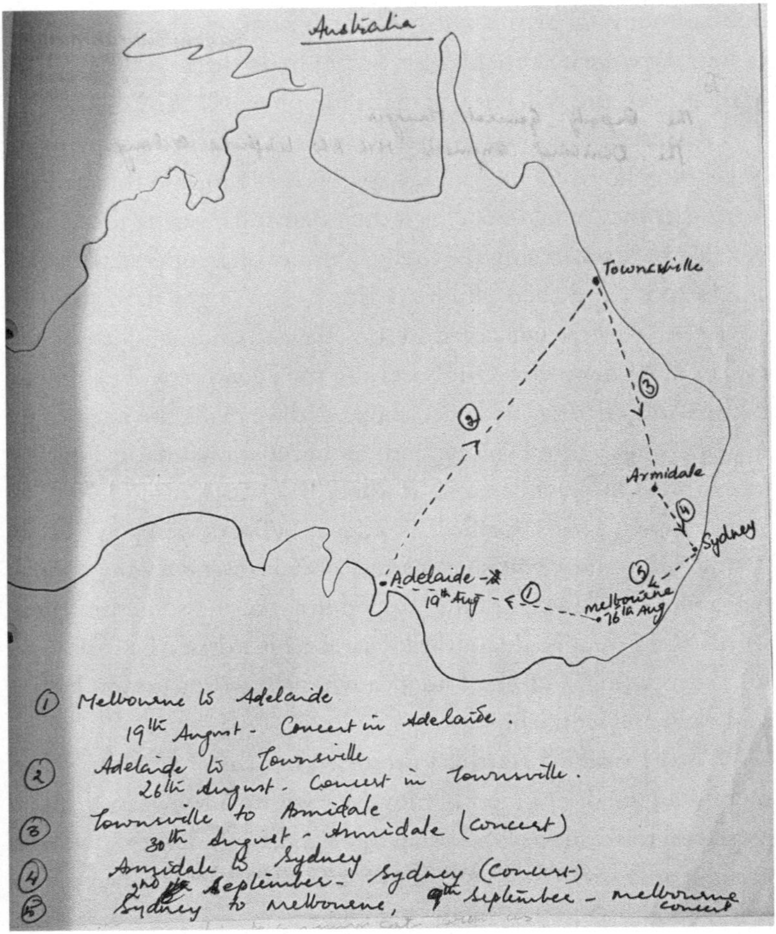

Aarthi's hand-drawn map of my tour of Australia

Two days before the first concert, we decided to go shopping. First, we went to the famous Globe Silk Stores. We looked for T-shirts, and there was nothing that cost less than eight ringgits. Back then Malaysian ringgit were worth about Rs 12. Aarthi began calculating in Indian rupees and was very upset with the prices. She lamented, 'See, you've brought me to a place where I can't even afford to buy a shirt right after marriage.' When the first concert got over, the sponsors gave me 300 ringgits. We went back to Globe. This time, we chanced on a T-shirt for four ringgits and thought, *oh that's a good price*. After the second concert, we looked at a nine-ringgit T-shirt in a different light too.

Until we actually had the money at hand, we had no idea of how much to spend. We were thinking in rupee terms. It was our first time, and we didn't know any better. We had no credit cards those days, so it was all cash transactions. Since we could bring only limited currency from home (there was a stringent limit on how much foreign exchange you could purchase in India in those days), it was hard to spend at first. Once the first pay trickled in, we began spending. By the third concert, we had started buying gifts for relatives too.

I went away on a long US tour for three months when Aarthi was pregnant with our second child and our first was just three-and-a-half years old. Phone calls were a complication, as well as a big expense, during foreign travel back in the day. By the early 2000s friends bought phone cards for me, say for US$ 10, so I could speak for about forty minutes. After the advent of the internet, calls became easier. Back when we didn't have laptops, we would go to people's home to use their PCs. But as soon as mobile phones came, I began carrying them constantly. In those years, during the tech boom, I was crazy about technology. I would go into stores like CompUSA, Best Buy or Fry's Electronics to check out new models of hard disks, routers and motherboards. I loved those shops. This was before online shopping became big, and you still had to shop in stores. Sometimes, I'd go just to look at the prices. My tech obsession also brought me to another lifelong interest, board games, thanks to the first ever podcast I heard. Soon enough, travelling meant hunting for fun new games (more on this later).

Until 2008, I continued to accept invitations to these long US tours, but then gradually reduced the time away from home to about five to six weeks. By 2010, I had cut it down to three weeks. When I first started performing in the US, there were concerts every Friday, Saturday and Sunday. From Monday through Thursday, we would wind down, completely exhausted. Of course, there was also the travel from one city to another, taking care of laundry from the week—I had to have well-ironed clothes for the concerts. There was nothing relaxing about the downtime. You'd just be in and out, doing your job. There was also the monotony that would set in during travels, and those dreaded standard questions. I'd try to limit social occasions but couldn't always escape them. Then there were the perils of being hosted by kind organisers. Some of them would have their kids sing for me, and I would need to find polite words of appreciation!

These days, it's a little better because I insist on staying in a hotel. It gives me some breathing space. I sing a concert, and then take a couple of days off to see a few things in these cities.

The big incentive for travelling to the US is, of course, getting to spend time with my two siblings. My brother Swaminathan aka Shyam is four-and-a-half years younger than me. He learnt Carnatic music from V. Lakshminarayana too—vocal, not the violin. Later, we both studied with my grandaunt until he quit and turned to mridangam under Kumbakonam Rajappa Iyer. He studied in IIT, Kharagpur and moved to the States in 1994, where he has lived since. He and his wife Anne, and my nieces Anjali and Meena are always in attendance whenever I perform in San Jose. Over the years, Anne has developed a good ear for Carnatic music, especially when sung by her brother-in-law! My sister Visalakshi aka Aarathi is eight-and-a-half years younger. My earliest practice sessions in singing were to put her to bed. She learnt the violin from Narayana Iyer, T.N. Krishnan's father, and later from M. Chandrasekharan. She lives in the US with her husband Bala, and my nephews Harikesan and Sundaresan. She is quite the Sanskrit pundit, and I surprised her once by tuning and singing a set of verses that she had composed in the language.

Happily for me, both my siblings enjoy listening to music and singing. Their spouses, in their own ways, have also supported and, I daresay, tolerated me over the years. Their kids grew up listening to a lot of my music and have embraced my newer ventures.

Talking to these kids has made me more sensitive to the world we live in. They're also my coaches on how the world works now. There was this comment on my Coke Studio song 'Elay Makka' that used the expression 'drip'. Nonplussed, I turned to Meena, who gave me the full lowdown on what it meant, and assured me that the younger generation actually approved of my look!

As the eldest child of both my parents, I am also the eldest cousin in our extended family. The cousin closest to me in age is Ram Nagarajan, and I've probably spent more time with him than anyone else. Over the years, he along with all my cousins have been a huge source of support in my musical journey. Our family gatherings tend to be vibrant, with banter and musical conversation drawing in not only immediate cousins but also extended grandaunts and granduncles, aunts and uncles, and numerous second and third cousins.

These days in the US, there's a well-oiled system for Carnatic music, closely following the Indian sabha culture. In certain places, such as Cleveland and San Diego, they promote music using the festival concept with two-day or three-day events. This gives their

A rare violin session

music scene a very predictable character. Often, the concerts are subsidised, with each town or city setting up a membership system to collect funds. These memberships are used to fund the artists, and they aim to provide as much music as possible to the local community. Typically, there are one or two big-ticket concerts, and then there are always close to eight smaller concerts. There are also a few promoters who organise these concerts, though none of it is done on a profit-sharing basis.

The crowds at these concerts over the years have stayed more or less constant. Ultimately, it is a big social occasion for the community. They come together, and if it's a big concert, more of them would like to be seen. And they are all interested in music; it's a solid show of support for the art form to help keep it going. Attending Carnatic concerts is also a way to communicate to their children that their family is still in contact with the mother country and in touch with our culture. Whether it's a Deepavali, Navaratri or Tamil Sangam concert, the audience comes in for all of these complex and intertwined reasons.

This is the standard model in most other countries. However, in Europe, the Sri Lankan Tamils have a separate subculture. There, the Tamil language is primary, and they hold Bharatanatyam in very high regard. The songs need to be in Tamil or the audience will switch off because of the language barrier. For them, language is important, not 'Carnatic music'. So when I sing in Tamil, these listeners are very into it. In fact, they relate strongly to and patronise all Tamil culture, be it literature, music, cinema or indie music.

Even through all this travel, the character of the audience has very rarely determined what I sing on stage. The exception was when, between 2006 and 2010, I performed a lot in Europe for the local audiences. Those concerts were always shorter, and you had to try and create highs in a brief span of about seventy-five minutes.

In longer concerts, you have the luxury of warming up slowly. Here, you had to wrap up in an hour. So, you were always on high alert. These shorter concerts helped me finally identify when and how the highs would come. Earlier, I would sing for a while, and then arrive at a big swaram or an RTP, and then perform a tukda to hit the crescendo. But after the short concert, I realised I could vary the ups and downs in the concert. As you are singing, different aspects of music provide scope for you to tinker with sound, so that the energy goes up or softens. More than the actual content, this has to do with the emotion and energy you bring to the table.

In a longer concert you are not pressured to create it in a hurry. But in shorter concerts, you have less time, so you have to be more conscious about how you work on those energy shifts. It's like playing a T20 match, in the second ball I have to go down the wicket.

The remotest place I've performed Carnatic music in was Denmark, where we crossed the sea from Hamburg and drove to a school where the concert was held. It was for a warm Sri Lankan Tamil audience, about a hundred of them came to listen to me, and I was happy to perform quite a few Tamil Carnatic songs. Travelling to these distant places and performing in front of audiences who may have never heard Carnatic music before offered me a glimpse into the power of art.

In March 1998, for instance, I was left speechless upon seeing a large poster of myself in a metro station in Paris. I had been invited to perform at the Théâtre de la Ville. Until then, I had never seen my photo in such a large format, and to witness it in Paris was electric.

The next time in Paris was an even bigger adventure. After another big concert at the Théâtre de la Ville, I had to travel to Correns in the south of France for the last concert of a month-long Europe tour. The train was at 7.15 a.m., a three-hour ride on the TGV speed rail from Paris to Aix-en-Provence. From there, it was an hour's drive to Correns. After we boarded, we found out that the café staff on the train were on strike, so no refreshments. Fortunately, I had bought some breakfast. That gave us the fuel to last the train ride.

We reached Aix-en-Provence at 10.30 a.m. and were picked up in a car. Halfway through the drive, our hosts realised that they had not picked up another musician who was due to perform at the venue as well. We went back to pick him up, and by the time we reached Correns, it was noon.

We had some good food waiting for us, and an hour's rest before the sound test at 1.30 p.m. It was bright and sunny and the venue was open-air. As we finished our sound test at 2 p.m., clouds suddenly began to gather. Our concert was only at 5 p.m., so we were not really worried. We roamed the streets of the quaint little village for a while and returned to rest before the performance. This was a music festival, and there were several bands and musicians. So the resting place was noisy as well, with musicians playing and singing. A jolly experience if you think about it, but not for those three weary travellers from India at that moment.

Meanwhile, the sky was getting darker, and the technicians started covering things up on stage. Now we did not know if they'd go ahead with our concert. It was a bit like a cricket match, with the skies darkening just before the start of play. At about 4.45 p.m., they decided that, since it had not started raining, they would go ahead with the concert. Then, just as we were about to step on to the stage, it began to pour. It had been dark, gloomy and chilly for three hours, but that was the moment the raindrops chose to fall.

Within ten minutes, an alternate venue was up, and impressively, the concert began with only a half-hour's delay. The wait and uncertainty had really made us nervous, with some of us resembling expectant fathers outside the maternity ward at Isabel's hospital in Chennai as we paced up and down, looking at the sky. The concert went off well, the audience was most gracious and accepting, and we had a good time on stage. As I finished a Kambhoji raga alapana, the audience was unsure whether to clap or not, whether that was the right moment. Just then, a young kid lying on his mother's lap led the way, launching into spontaneous applause.

We finished dinner, drove back through a long-winding mountain road on a full stomach, clutching our intestines as the driver took fast turns in a speedy Peugeot van, reminding us of a ride from Kotagiri to Coonoor in a Matador van. We reached the station and caught the train to reach Paris at about 1 a.m. and flopped onto our beds bed at about 2 a.m., exhausted.

Back in 2003, ahead of a concert in Spain, in a small town called Caravaca, during a sound test, Varadarajan was playing Neelambari. The sound technician, who had never heard Carnatic music, said that it sounded to him like a lullaby. I have never forgotten this—he had never heard Carnatic music before, yet the sound of Neelambari was to him a lullaby. That year, I also had the unique experience of singing at midnight for both the Sivarathri in Chennai and Easter in Spain.

Good food is an abiding love; I'm a sucker for it. When I travel, I avoid Indian food. You get the best Indian food here at home, in India. So, when I go on a tour to Chicago, and someone says, 'Do you want to eat idlis? You must be missing it,' I say, 'Trust me, I don't.' To be fair, back in the day, artists who used to travel couldn't adapt to foreign foods, and the hosts in these countries are primed to being attentive to their visitors' needs. But since I travel so extensively, I've adapted to all kinds of food. (Although one Sunday a month, if I'm in Chennai, I like to go out to a restaurant and have pongal-vada!)

Rama Varma is a fellow foodie who loves introducing my family to new food. If he knows I am singing a concert in Bombay, and there's a restaurant that we plan on trying there, he'll say, 'I will come to Bombay, we'll go and eat there.' Anytime he finds a new restaurant in Chennai, he'll come home and take us. He also brings food souvenirs from his travels for us, and we do the same for him, especially chocolates and rare desserts.

I have a group of friends who are also connoisseurs of whiskies and wines. In Australia, I enjoy sampling the local beers, and when I travel, I make it a point to visit wine distilleries for tasting sessions. What I actually appreciate the most in these spaces is the unique food-and-drink pairings. I walked into a winery in Niagara on a recent trip, and while the wine was underwhelming, the food was fantastic. In Vegas, it's not the casinos but the vibrant restaurant scene and live shows that have my heart. Theatre, musicals, magic shows, the circus or sports, I love watching anything live while travelling. I also visit museums to catch art shows whenever I can. Raja uncle, a quintessential London gentleman of Sri Lankan Tamil origin and a distinguished member of the Royal Academy, always ensured I caught an exhibit or two when I went to London. This macintosh-wearing patron of Carnatic music, would not only host me at the best restaurants in London, but he was also the first to take me to see Monet, Rembrandt and Van Gogh in person.

CHAPTER 10

The Making and Re-making of My Aesthetic

I like to start my concerts with a smile, I can't help but smile even while singing. I don't like to be morose—it's not my temperament. What am I doing on stage, anyway, if not performing? Engagement with the audience is crucial to me. I make eye contact. Even when there were fewer listeners at my concerts, I liked to look at those who were listening keenly or were nodding in appreciation. Now, while singing in a studio, I look at the cameraperson, especially if they acknowledge the music. Ultimately, an artistic performance is about creating, sharing and experiencing something together. It is, in a sense, a community effort, where a group of people come together, forget about everything else in their lives for those few hours and go back home feeling satisfied. I'm not looking to make people feel anything beyond just this. This much I can promise, anything else the audience feels is their own takeaway for that day.

As I see it, I've remained consistent with what I have to offer, aligning with mainstream conventions for a Carnatic music performance. There is a well-settled formula, and I have adhered to it as it has been practised for the last hundred years, with perhaps minor tweaks here and there. I do make small changes, such as the manner in which I sing or the amount of time I spend singing swara, for instance. Compared to thirty years ago, I might sing more Tamil songs on some days and more Kannada songs on others, but there hasn't been a dramatic change in my aesthetic choices since those early years.

When I sing on stage now, the way I use my voice and the manner in which I elaborate a raga is evolving. This aspect is nebulous because I enjoy unpredictability. However, when I sing a composition, most parts of the song remain unchanged. I stick to what I have always done. You can take a rendition of a particular song from 1986 and compare it to the same song in 2024, and you will find that around 80 per cent of how I've sung on both occasions remains the same. In this sense, I can be called predictable, or consistent, and I enjoy that too. At the same time, the creative elements in the song keep changing, introducing a 10–20 per cent unpredictability in my performance.

All of this is to say, I have been conservative and consistent, like most performers. Yet, I have also always been spontaneous in my creative bursts. I have never been afraid of taking risks on stage. When these risks pay off, it's thrilling as a performer, and the listener gets to participate in that moment of shared creation.

Risk-taking in a classical concert basically involves attempting something I have not sung at home or anytime in the past. The risk in this is, of course, I don't know where it's going to lead me. This is a great thrill. It is my innate nature, this curiosity. (Or if you believe in Linda Goodman, it's apparently what Aquarians do.) Even when I drive, I like to try new routes. This is just an extension of that personality trait.

When I did this over time, I stopped being scared, which is one of the biggest challenges that performers face. *How much risk can I take?* Of course, I can always choose to sing something safe, rasikas will like it. *What do I get out of this?* It's just a high, something personal. I am pushing some boundary inside myself to get something new out of the experience. This spontaneity comes rarely and is special when it happens in a classical concert. And it doesn't come solely from the content of one's music but also from one's personality. I keep asking myself what it is that I experience the most in each moment as I sing and what I wish to convey to the audience the most. The answer has invariably been 'joy'.

While performing, I feel nothing short of happiness, I feel a rush. Even if the song or lyric is sad, there's always an inner feeling of joy that drives me, and that translates into my music. It is my primary emotion when I sing, everything else is secondary.

Joy in art, however, is not frivolity. Nor is it divorced from the seriousness of craft. The late educationist Rajalakshmi Parthasarathy (who founded the famous PSBB group of schools in Chennai) would always give the founder's vote of thanks in Bharat Kalachar. One year, in the late 1990s, she addressed me in her speech and said, 'Sanjay, you used to be such a playful young boy on stage. Now, you've become a serious vidwan.' She then said it at every vote of thanks she gave for eight years afterwards. I think it's because she remembered me from when I was young: a not-so-serious twenty-three-year-old, who was prone to cracking jokes, being more angry or more funny—more of everything, for that matter. Then she saw me turn serious all of a sudden. It's true that there was a clear shift in my attitude. I think it had to do with becoming a professional and having people pay money to listen to me. That made a huge difference in my mind, the evening slot. *Why are they spending money to come and listen to you? You have a job, you have a responsibility. You can't be frivolous. You have to deliver value for their money and time, though you can't measure art that way, you cannot compromise on quality in any manner.* That was how I felt about it.

❦

The other aesthetic choice that can make or break a performance is your onstage company. In the early years, you cannot really choose; usually, three of your friends accompany you to all your concerts. Friendship drives those performances. However, as a professional, you are required to develop a readiness to sing with anybody. If someone calls from Kerala, you go and sing with whoever is available or whoever the organiser has chosen. There is no choice in the matter. Only after you've grown and gained an audience are you asked for your preference. That's the time to make a studied choice.

This choice hinges on two factors: first, does it help how you are perceived on stage, and, second, how much better does your concert become with a particular accompanist? It is a personal judgement. *If these people perform with me, my concert will be good for me or for my audience.* For instance, if a senior musician accompanies me, even if age has slowed them down, their brand offers significant value. I'll be able to make it work and sing with them. The performance may not be perfect, but it will add something unique to the concert.

That special something could even be the chemistry between a vocalist and an accompanist. Like when Guruvayur Dorai played for me, the violinist Mysore Nagaraj told me, 'He has been playing with so many people; but with you he plays differently.' Of course, I too give a 100 per cent to whoever plays with me. There is no ego. I don't look around the stage and feel, *Why the hell am I sitting with this person?* T.K. Moorthy, Palghat Raghu and Vellore Ramabhadran, as I've mentioned earlier, were the three senior mridangam maestros who accompanied me early in my career and provided tremendous encouragement. As a young singer in the nineties, sharing the stage with these stalwarts was a huge boost to my career. They were always eager to perform and never made any demands, whether commercial or musical. I also owe a great deal to violinists Thiruparkkadal Veeraraghavan, Sikkil Bhaskaran and V. Thiagarajan. These artists not only played alongside me but also offered invaluable musical insights during travels, suggesting compositions and musical phrases that I could incorporate into my own music. TVG is a significant source of inspiration and support. Every few months over the past five or six years, I have visited him, spent a couple of hours together and left feeling recharged and inspired.

After the pandemic, I insisted that Varadarajan and Venkatesh play with me. By this time, we had reached a point where it felt like we were almost a band, or brand, however you look at it. I was ready to turn down a programme if I wasn't playing with them. After singing with several artists, and performing numerous concerts, you learn that you are comfortable with certain people, and working with some people is beneficial to your own performance.

Many factors influence this feeling, such as who you are comfortable travelling with, or whether there's a match in professional dealings and whom you trust. Once I made the decision, it was as if we were a family. It helps that they are both at their peak!

Varadarajan was a child superstar. He's five years younger than me. When I started out as a singer at nineteen, he was fourteen and already playing concerts. Big concerts. He was very popular. People admired him. *Such a young boy playing so well.* Even then, he had a very sharp brain, and could play anything after listening to it just once. He performed with me for the first time in 1993 in Kochi and has been a regular accompanist since.

When I moved to the evening slot at the Music Academy, Varadarajan remained in the afternoon slot for another year. Upset, he said, 'I won't play this year.'

I told him, 'You play this year in the afternoon slot. Next year, I will make sure you are promoted.'

Then I fought for him. He was so good, and I felt that the Academy was being unjust to him.

He's a brilliant musician, with absolutely no ego on stage, skilfully adjusting to my sudden exploits while singing. Other violinists tended to get upset with the kind of liberties I took on stage in wanting to be spontaneous, but Varadu was and is a good sport. Even when I try something new and do not succeed, he takes it in his stride and tries again. This makes for friendly banter on stage, and also gives our concert a good effect. It has been like that between us for a long time.

For instance, when I am elaborating a raga, when I sing a phrase, Varadu repeats after me. The manner of his playing sometimes determines how my next phrase pans out. So, there is a continuum that is unfolding, and it is not rehearsed because he doesn't know what I'm going to sing next. Sometimes, when he is in good form and he's responding strongly, I'll push him more and more, and then a while later I'll decide, okay that's enough, let me go into a zone with my own singing. The moment I do that, he'll take a back seat, just playing along and allowing me to go through with my thought process. It's the same when I perform swarams too. This is largely an unspoken equation. We don't sit down to plan it, but over the years, we have managed to establish a pattern. That is the synergy we share.

The other constant at my concerts is Venkatesh, whom I initially knew only through Arun Prakash. Arun mentioned to me once that his guru's student, Venkatesh, could play the kanjira. I sent him a letter inviting him to play with me as there was no telephone at his home—that's how it used to be in those days. Venkatesh joined us for a concert in Nellore for the first time. For about five years, he played the kanjira at my concerts. However, he was also starting to play the mridangam then.

At the Thyagaraja Utsavam in Chicago in 1998, there were two concerts, one by Shashank and another by me. Both concerts had the same set of accompanists booked, including Ganesh Prasad, Neyveli Venkatesh and Karthik. I was impressed by Venkatesh's mridangam playing, and started performing regularly with him. We later performed together on tours in Europe and the US.

Once, when Guruvayur Dorai played the mridangam for me on a tour, even though Venkatesh had already started performing as a mridangist, he came along on the full tour to play kanjira at my request. Since then, we have worked together regularly.

Venkatesh is like a metronome on stage. I don't need to think about rhythm because he travels perfectly in sync with my singing. When he plays along during the songs, my improvisations for the kalpanaswaram seem to flow uninhibitedly. And when he gets his ten-minute solo, he electrifies the concert. The atmosphere becomes charged by the time he finishes.

What Venkatesh typically does, and it works beautifully, is he lands on a tempo depending on how I'm singing. When he feels that I'm reaching the crescendo, he'll reach for the same, and seeing his rising tempo, I'll go farther. We feed off each other's energy on stage, and then when it reaches this place where I know neither of us can go on, I'll hold back. All of this is very visible up on the stage. People know exactly when we're taking it up a notch. And then there are those songs where there is no need for anybody to do anything. Both of us like to render them quietly in perfect balance, so that the song's magic can stand on its own. None of us has to do a thing extra.

On stage, both Varadu and Venkatesh go above and beyond to ensure the concert's success; they also make sure to shine in the

A lighter moment with the men in white

ten minutes that are exclusively theirs; and the entire time I'm performing with them, I feel reassured that they are there, no matter what. Most accompanists are like that, but with us now it feels more special because of the way things have worked out for years. Every time we are on stage together, I know we're watching out for each other.

Venkatesh has also ended up influencing the visual aesthetics of my concerts. Now, all of us perform in white. He was the original man in white, having worn only whites at concerts for years. I wore various colours in the beginning and then gradually moved towards cream, off-white and sandalwood shades. Eventually I stopped wearing kurtas; they felt uncomfortable since I was a bit heavier back then. I felt that half-sleeved shirts were more comfortable, like the Thanjavur zilla shirts that became popular when the Tamil film *Chinna Gounder* released.

When I decided to move from kurtas to shirts, Aarthi declared, 'You must wear only white.' Given how much I perspire through the course of a concert, Aarthi jokes that, like a tennis player, I need to change my clothes in the middle of a match. This is also why white cottons make the most sense. Coincidentally, as we were deciding to go with shirts, someone we know gifted me a bale of white fabric. Soon, I developed a deep interest in Ponduru cottons. These veshtis from Andhra are very soft, ideal for concerts.

Varadarajan used to wear coloured shirts for a while, but then he too started wearing whites. Venkatesh then offered to take us all to the place he sources his cotton shirts and veshtis from. The entire thing unfolded very organically. Younger musicians have asked me, 'How big is your wardrobe?' because they don't know if I am managing with four white shirts or forty.

It only took the audience twenty years to catch on and finally call us 'the men in white', and for us to use that to promote a concert. I joke that it's like the Chinese magician in the film *The Prestige*, who pretends to be a cripple all his life for the sake of that one fishbowl act!

Of course, this was an aesthetic call too. Inspiration came from my heroes—GNB, who donned all-whites, and Palghat Mani Iyer's khadi shirts that the man famously apparently starched himself!

Over the years, my concert repertoire has also undergone significant transformation, adding another layer to my changing aesthetic. I am no longer singing many songs that I performed in my early years. The number of keerthanams I sing has come down, for instance. Pre-recorded concerts, which I had to perform as a result of the lockdown, were instrumental in developing this new repertoire.

Since I tried to incorporate at least one Kannada song in my line-up every month, for instance, my existing song stock was quickly depleted. I had to work diligently to avoid repetition. I began performing songs I hadn't sung before. All of these explorations spilt over into my post-pandemic live performances too.

However, the most profound change was in my newfound willingness to sing anything, so long as it excites me. I do not want to be bound by genre anymore. I am a Carnatic singer. People call me a Carnatic musician. There is always this genre prefix associated with my name, even if I choose to call myself a singer. While I cannot shake off the association entirely, I do want to slowly build a body of work that showcases me in a different light.

Breaking the mould in terms of what I sing and using my voice differently has been an interesting and enjoyable process. *Anbenum Peruveli* was a big breakthrough musically as well as artistically for me. All the songs in the album evolved democratically. Sean was the composer, but the whole band worked together on every song. While the final call on what went into the song was his, we all worked to get there, contributing to the various musical elements of the song. From here, I want to move on to the next stage, where I create or write songs myself instead of relying on existing texts. I have previously composed a number of tunes, written a little in Tamil—single liners for pallavis—but this album, and what it might bring next, is creatively exciting.

All my life, I have thought alone and I have sung alone. Now I find myself seized by the spirit of collaboration; finding new ideas, working with other minds, especially younger ones.

In your younger years, you look up to older people and learn from them, you want to emulate them. When you grow older, you look at young people and want to do what they are doing. I am careful about not unsettling the youngsters I like working with and avoid forcing my personality on them. Maintaining this balance is my current challenge.

You don't want to be this boomer whose calls they are scared of receiving. My children have taught me how to avoid doing just this. When you learn how to interact with your children, you learn to interact with everybody.

CHAPTER 11

Life Off the Stage

My interests in things besides classical music has helped me forge a community that I share my life and days off stage with. Cricket, as you might have guessed, has been a constant throughout my life. It was the first sport I fell in love with.

My dad was a sports fanatic and introduced me to the joys of reading the sports page of *The Hindu*. Discussions on the day's news, scores and team selections dominated our daily conversations. He was also a longtime bridge player, though none of us picked up the game. He taught us swimming and took us to cricket matches at Chepauk.

In the early days, before television came to India, I listened to radio commentary broadcasts. My first memory of cricket was a Tamil Nadu vs Karnataka Ranji match in 1974. I was about six then, but I still remember who played and scored what. Radio was my window to the cricketing world. My dad was, of course, an avid listener, particularly to two series. During the English summer, he would tune in to the BBC shortwave broadcasts. On December mornings, he would listen to Australia's matches on ABC Radio. Appa usually woke up a bit later, but if he was up at 5.30 or 6 a.m., you could be sure it was December or January, and that he'd be listening to the Australian Test matches commentary. These early-morning sessions became a part of our family routine during the cricket season.

Commentary played a huge role in my interest in cricket. I played gully cricket, of course, and tried my hand at school-level cricket, but I was a failed cricketer. I neither practised enough nor had the talent. At best, I was an enthusiast—a role I embraced with gusto, from rigorously following the game's statistics to reading a lot of scorecards. As soon as I received the latest issue of *Sportsweek* or *Sportstar*, I would turn to the scorecard page.

I followed the writers in *Sportstar* religiously, becoming a fan of many of their writing styles and always looking forward to their insights. Brian Glanville, for instance, wrote regularly about football. From one of his articles, I learnt that he had written a novel about a British footballer going to Italy and playing there. Intrigued, I went to the British Council Library and borrowed the very enjoyable *The Rise of Gerry Logan*.

Every morning, I'd open *The Hindu* and look for county cricket scores, which the newspaper published in those days. I liked to keep a tab on who was playing for which county. When Sunil Gavaskar played for Somerset, I began to follow their scorecard as well. And though I've always liked Gavaskar and Kapil Dev, my big hero back then was Gundappa Vishwanath, especially after his famous ninety-seven-not-out innings in Madras. I was at the stadium that day and even have some memories of it. My brother and I watched all five days of the Chennai Tied Test in 1986. Outside of Madras, the only place I've watched a test match is at the Oval in London during the Ashes. It was great fun. Now, whenever I travel, if there is a sport I can watch live, I try to catch it—perhaps there isn't a sport you cannot interest me in. I keep up with hockey during the Asian Games. Tennis grand slams, especially Wimbledon, have been a longtime favourite. I've also always loved collecting sports trivia, details like who won how many gold medals at different Asian Games. Over the years, I've caught basketball, soccer, football, rugby and ice hockey matches live during my travels abroad for kutcheris.

These days, I follow soccer, and during the World Cup, I watch football closely. A long time ago, when I was in Australia, a friend suggested I follow Arsenal. Back then, I enjoyed watching Thierry Henry play for the team. Over the last five years, my son has become a big Tottenham Hotspur fan. I've started supporting Arsenal again now, possibly out of a desire to forge a sporting connection with him. Though I don't follow the scene regularly, I still engage with it and even play a bit of crypto fantasy football on the blockchain. There is a website called Sorare, which allows you to play fantasy football using cryptocurrency where each player is an NFT. This year, I even found myself following a Spanish second division team, Santander, because I've performed a kutcheri there.

My friends Shrikanth and Mohan, now in Canada and Australia respectively, became close friends during my first tour of Australia and the US in 1995. I always think of them as a duo because I met them both that year. Mohan was in Melbourne and Srikanth in New Mexico. We've been friends for almost thirty years, an integral part of my inner circle. Over the years, their families and ours have bonded over a shared love of sports, travel, films, books, food and board games. Mohan and Girija, Srikanth and Vasumathi—these friendships have given me much joy.

Every music season, they stay at my house and attend all my concerts. We are all about the same age, share a strong interest in sports and watch some games together while they are here. Varadarajan follows cricket as well, so he's usually a part of this gang. Venkatesh, on the other hand, is a contrarian. If we all support CSK, he'll back the other nine teams. If we support India in the World Cup, he'll root for the other fifteen teams. It makes for good banter and keeps our conversations fun.

V.K. Shankar is another close and dear friend whom I've mentioned earlier in the context of his grandfather, V.S. Gomathi Sankara Iyer. Shankar and his wife Kavitha are more than just friends; they're our travel buddies. We've shared countless holidays together.

Many of our current travel adventures involve one of these three couples. The thing about friends is that the relationship ebbs and flows over time. Yet, the bond remains, ready to be rekindled whenever we meet again. For instance, I have these wonderful friends in Dayton, Ohio—Mali, Nalini and their kids. Earlier, I would visit Dayton every time I was in the States, creating fond memories with each trip.

At this stage of life, I have many memories to look back on, and much to look forward to. I feel like I'm at a midpoint, with old and new friends moulding this journey just as much as my family does. Younger artists like Sean Roldan and the stand-up comedian Aravind S.A. bring a refreshing youthful energy into our lives, adding another layer of richness to our experiences.

Appa's influence brought another abiding interest into my life early on—reading. He was a well-read man, and introduced me early on to Shakespeare and Wodehouse. He was also a theatre actor, and wrote scripts for my siblings and me to enact during Bala Vihar celebrations. I began by reading a read a lot of comics—Hot Stuff, Marvel, Justice League, Asterix, Tintin—then Enid Blyton, Hardy Boys, Nancy Drew, suchlike. When I reached middle school, I began reading westerns, Louis L'Amour and Max Brand. By the time I was in the ninth standard, all my friends were reading Nick

Carter and James Hardley Chase. Appa asked disapprovingly, 'What is this? Why are you reading all this now?' So, I used to hide those books from everyone at home and read them.

The librarian at St Bedes school, an older Anglo-Indian gentleman, had a big influence on my reading habits. Since I was a constant presence at the library, he once asked me if I'd read Greek mythology. When I said no, he picked out a book for me. When he figured out that I actually read his suggestions, he began to introduce more books to me. That's how I came to read about Achilles, for instance.

'Have you read Shakespeare?' he asked once, and without waiting for a reply, handed me a book and said, 'Take this.' It was Shakespeare for children.

My reading has always been eclectic. I read footnotes, forewords, prefaces, and these lead me to newer authors. I love going down rabbit holes. In a second-hand bookstore, for instance, I saw a book about a spy scandal involving the four Cambridge spies, Donald Maclean, Guy Burgess, Kim Philby and Anthony Blunt. When I finished reading it, I realised they had inspired John LeCarré's books. These are the most rewarding kinds of revelations, ones that leave me looking forward to my next book. The aunt who suggested I write this book, Shobha—married to my musical uncle Suresh—is a former director of Penguin India with an eclectic taste in literature and art. She introduced me to classic writers like Anthony Trollope and Thomas Mann.

The more I read, the more I grow as a human being; the more I see of this world through the eyes of other people, the more I change, understand how the world works. The antidote to the disregard for the value of human life is, in fact, art in its myriad forms, as it evokes empathy and introspection.

As I've mentioned before, my initiation into Tamil literature began as an attempt to assuage an inferiority complex about not having read enough in my mother tongue. I went through this phase where I would read everything I could lay my hands on. Books by Thi. Janakiraman, Sundara Ramasamy, Yuvan Chandrashekar (who would also constantly suggest writers for me to read and even lend me some of his books), G. Nagarajan, Ku. Pa. Ra., Mowni, Ki Rajanarayanan, Cho Dharman, Poomani, Jeyamohan, S. Ramakrishnan, Pudhumaipithan, Sujatha, Devan, Suresh Kumar Indrajith, Imayam, Ambai, Perumal Murugan. For almost a decade, I read Tamil obsessively. More than the influence it had on my music, I think reading all those books ended up sensitising me as a human being in a very big way, because it exposed me to a wide variety of Tamil subcultures that I was completely oblivious to. I'd lived all my life in Madras, in Mylapore, a privileged urban setting. Reading Tamil allowed me access to other lives. Today, I'm able to look at everything from society to politics through my understanding of these other worlds gleaned from books. Even when it's fiction, the stories I read are deeply rooted in the spaces these writers are living in. This is the joy of reading literature that doesn't originate in the English. You can glimpse these stories in films too, but it's literature that leaves the deeper mark. The understanding you get from reading cuts deeper somehow.

Interestingly, it is Tamil literature that brought me to literary fiction, especially translations, in English. I'd never read the likes of Umberto Eco and Gabriel García Márquez. I'd read the names of writers like Borges and Márquez in Tamil novels. That's how I came to read *One Hundred Years of Solitude*, and then read Milan Kundera and Mario Vargas Llosa.

While I do enjoy reading fiction, I have to confess to being partial to non-fiction. Anything that's of interest to me, I like to chase down a book or two on it and read. During the course of listening to William Dalrymple's Empire podcast, I read books on colonisation and the Partition, and have now bought some books on slavery, which were also mentioned in the podcast. I collect and read sports biographies of course.

*

Growing up, I played a lot of board games—trading games, cards, chess, carrom board and the like. But I'd completely lost touch with them as I grew up. Around 2005, when podcasts were just coming up in a big way, I bought an iPod. Being a tech enthusiast, I wanted to download some tech podcasts to listen to. Among the top five podcasts was something called Geek Speak. I downloaded it and then realised that they were board-game geeks, not tech geeks. When I heard the podcast, though, I was intrigued by the number of games they were talking about. I got home from a concert in Madurai, which is where I heard that first podcast, and visited their website. There were 30,000 board games mentioned on it! I was completely drawn into their world. I began playing and buying games, and even sourcing them from outside India. I used to have people over just to play, then my kids started playing, and soon enough all our friends began playing board games. I used to play some cricket once in a while, and those friends too started playing board games with me. Now I have about 450 board games at home, taking over the walls of an entire room. I haven't bought many new games recently, but I did play a lot of board games during the pandemic. And the community of people I play with keeps growing. I log all the players I've played with, who wins what, and the scores. I have an app to do that, and my game h-index is 38 (which basically means I've played thirty-eight games at least thirty-eight times). I've played some games 200 times as well!

Just as I was beginning to feel a little upset that my family had sort of given up on board games, I happened to buy a table which had a secret compartment. That compartment had a collection

Gaming as a young family

of stamps in a stamp book. This started a philately hobby that I maintained for about ten years. I tried collecting stamps around themes as well. I found stamps around the life and work of this Czech composer called Bedřich Smetana, but then I never got to finish it. I am still a member of Motivgruppe Musik group that does musical philately. They send me a magazine every quarter. One day, I went on their website and was pleasantly surprised to find my photograph alongside Yehudi Menuhin's in their 'prominent musician members' section.

I collected postcards too for some time, and would also do something called post-crossing, where I would send a postcard with a stamp to a foreign country, and someone else would send me one with one of their stamps. Since I did this in my daughter's name, she eventually laid claim to that collection. My son insisted that he wanted some collection in his name, so Aarthi started him off on numismatics. There is still a little box in my house with the coins Aarthi and he collected.

And then I went through a comic book phase. I used to go around second-hand book stores to find comics. I have about forty fountain pens. I have done all kinds of things to collect them, including going all the way to Thiruvallur once to buy Indian ebonite pens from Ranga Pens. I use these mainly to write notations. But at one point, I thought my handwriting was going bad, and I started writing a diary with these fountain pens. Even now, I write sporadically.

As my hobbies make evident, I am a hoarder by nature. I love collecting things, recording things and archiving them. I still have a box of old invitation letters from sabhas, another one has newspaper cuttings of articles, especially during the December season. I have a box of pre-recorded cassettes and CDs. I have a box of theatre playbills from shows that I have watched. I even have a box of my early travel tickets and boarding passes. I had a large library that I have trimmed down a lot now.

Just as I log every board-game session, I also log every kind of whisky or wine that I drink. There's an app I record this on, and even rate them. For a while, I noted down every song I ever practised date-wise. I had a blog where I reviewed board games. Once, when I commented on some board-game forum, a user observed that I am a musician and shared a link to one of my videos. That was fun! I had a Tamil blog for some time and a cricket blog for a while. In the early years of the internet, I was everywhere. Even now, if you look, you'll find my comments littered all over message boards and blogs. I sometimes wonder why I try and record or archive everything. Perhaps it comes from my love for history. Archiving, in particular, has taught us so much about the past and how humanity has evolved. It's also a chance to leave things for someone in the distant future to try and understand what we were doing now. It also feels nice to revisit these and see how I have changed and evolved.

Finally, it was the pandemic that really brought about a change in my family's hoarding habits. We now like to spend that time and money on experiences. As I write this, I am planning a trip to Bombay to go and see a Gulam Mohammed Sheikh retrospective.

Through all of this, if there's an interest that has served me well over the years on and off the stage, it is strength training. When I put on a lot of weight, I suffered immensely at concerts, because the increased weight brought on knee pain. When I finally met Basu Shanker of Primal Patterns, who is a former BCCI strength and conditioning coach and has worked with Team India, he put me on a proper regimen of strength training and a diet that included a good deal of protein. My daughter soon joined Basu to work as a strength coach and has since been helping me. I work out very regularly, religiously. It helps me not just with weight issues, but also with my health in general. Travel does get in the way, and I try to walk while on tour, but when I come back home, I always go back to working out. I am better off now than I was twenty years ago, when I was not just huge but also felt very unfit.

I am a 'now and today' kind of person, not someone who like to hark back to past traditions—a mindset that makes my ventures outside of Carnatic music feel natural to me. As a person, I strive to be as liberal as I can be. Human society is constantly evolving, and I want to evolve with it. What I read at different times also influences how I think and perceive the world. Though I don't have any grand illusions that I'm here to change the world, my focus is on engaging with my immediate circle and people I meet with in my personal life in a reasonable manner, free from preconceived notions, prejudices or insensitivity.

My relationship with my music too is deeply personal. While I do not shy away from acknowledging that the content I sing is primarily Hindu religious music, it is also a fact that I relate to these songs on my own terms. Each song, whether by Thyagaraja or Dikshitar, holds a significance in my life. When I perform these songs publicly, I have no agenda beyond singing itself. Either it resonates with listeners, or it doesn't. But I'm loath to pontificate on religion or spirituality just because I sing. Religion, in my view, is largely a sociopolitical experience, and I find myself only at its fringes, as my primary connection to society is through my music. As for spirituality, I'd like to reiterate what I said in an interview with the Tamil magazine *Vikatan*. Spirituality is deeply personal, something each person must experience on their own. It's not something I can talk about, nor can I claim that everyone who listens to Carnatic music feels spiritual. After all, I'm not a seer, a saint, a guru, or a philosopher—I'm just a singer.

As such, I am very shy, but not on stage, because that's my domain. How I am on stage ends as I exit the stage. The moment I'm out of the auditorium and in the car, I try not to carry 'it' with me. I'm just another guy off the stage. I like walking to places. I do get stopped once in a while, and people talk to me if they see me, but that's it. If I have work in the passport office or need to have a form filled, I'll go quietly stand in a queue and wait for my turn.

For as long as I can remember, I've liked being part of a team. My natural instinct is not to be the leader, I'd rather be the number two or three guy. I like to play the role of a mentor of sorts. Come to me, I'll tell you my thoughts, and then you can do as you please, but I won't say I am going to show the way. This has worked well for me. When I sing with four other people in a Coke Studio song, people ask me, 'Why are you doing all this at this stage of your career?' But I am going there of my own volition, keeping aside all other ideas of who I am. I want to be among these people.

My life in music, and the one outside it, is enriched by my chosen family. For my own family, including my brothers and cousins, I am not just Sanjay Subrahmanyan, the Carnatic singer. To my elders, I'm still the kiddo they knew. And my contemporaries will still pull my leg the first opportunity they get.

All of this is to say, once I exit the stage, I am just me. And I like that.

Glossary

alapana	Exploration of a raga unbound by beat (or talam), employing syllables such as ta, da, ri, na
apaswara	Off-key
charanam	The verse of a composition
gamaka	The oscillation or ornamentation of a note
gandharam	The 'ga' note, which is the third note in the Carnatic solfa scale
gurukulam	System of learning from a teacher by boarding in his/her house
janta varisai	Beginner's scale exercise involving repeating solfa syllables, such as 'sa, sa'; 'ri ri', etc.
kalpanaswaram	Improv singing of notes that land on a particular line of the composition. This is done over several rounds
kanakku	Means 'arithmetic' in Tamil. In Carnatic music, it refers to rhythmic patterns employed in improv singing
keerthanam	A compositional form, which usually has a chorus and verses

korappu	Means 'to reduce' in Tamil. In Carnatic music, it refers to an improvisational exercise where musicians exchange volleys of extempore kalpanaswarams of fewer and fewer bars
korvai	Also called a 'mukthayam', a korvai is a complex rhythmic pattern employed at the end of a round of improvisation. It is usually sung or played three times, in patterns of threes
krithi	Often used interchangeably with keerthanam
kutcheri	A live Carnatic concert
madhyamam	The 'ma' note, which is the fourth note in the Carnatic solfa scale
manodharma	Improvisational music
misra chapu	A musical cycle of seven beats
Music Academy	A music organisation, primarily focused on Carnatic music and Bharatanatyam dance, based in Chennai.
Kamalamba Navavarnam	A set of nine compositions of Muthuswami Dikshitar on Goddess Kamalamba, a form of Parvathi.
nishada swaram/ nishadam	The 'ni' note, which is the ninth note in the Carnatic solfa scale.
pallavi	The chorus of a composition or a part of the RTP
panchamam	The 'pa' note, which is the fifth note in the Carnatic solfa scale

Ragam Tanam Pallavi/RTP	A form that explores one or more ragas in detail through three kinds of improvisation: the ragam, an alapana; the tanam, improvisation using the syllables 'ta' and 'nam', with no strict rhythm but has a pulse; the pallavi, a single-line composition, often in an unusual talam with an underlying rhythmic idea.
ragamalika swaram	A kalpanaswaram performed in a string of ragas, instead of a single raga
rishabam	The 'ri' note, which is the second note in the Carnatic solfa scale
sabha	Organisers of Carnatic music and Bharatanatyam dance concerts, who may or may not own their own venue
sangathi	The same line of a song sung in different variations
sarali varisai	The first scale exercise taught to students of Carnatic music
Season/Music Season/ December Season	A series of concerts, lecture demonstrations, dance and drama performances organised by sabhas across Chennai in December, mostly during the Tamil month of Margazhi beginning in the latter half of December
shadja	The 'sa' note, which is the first note in the Carnatic solfa scale
spool tape	A precursor to the audio cassette, using a wider, larger magnetic tape to record and reproduce sounds

sruthi box	A reed-based instrument used to provide a drone of the shadjam ('sa') and panchamam ('pa') to accompany singing
swarakshara	When the syllable in the composition is the same as the solfa syllable. For example, in M. Balamuralikrishna's 'Hanuma anuma …' every 'ma' in the song is a 'ma' note
swarajati	A composition consisting of a pallavi, and different charanams, where each note has a corresponding lyric. It is usually taught to beginners, after scale exercises and simple compositions called geetham, and before varnams
swaras	Could refer to a note, or be used as a shorthand for kalpanaswarams
thalam	A cycle of beats in which a composition is set
Thyagaraja Aradhana	A festival in memory of eighteenth-century Carnatic composer Thyagaraja, held at his birthplace, Thiruvaiyaru, on his death anniversary
tisram	Rhythmic triplets
tukda	Smaller, lighter compositions sung usually at the end of a Carnatic concert
varnam	A composition of lyric and solfa syllables, often sung at the beginning of a concert
virutham	Improvised singing of poetry not set to rhythm, exploring a raga or a series of ragas. The lyric used is often a religious sloka, although it does not necessarily have to be so

9 789360 459673

Printed at Repro India Ltd.